The Pilgrim Virgin Statue Church to Home Visitation

To Establish the Reign of the Sacred Heart of Jesus in the Home and Bring Us Closer to Him in the Holy Eucharist

by First Saturdays for Peace

Unless otherwise stated, the Scripture quotations are from *The Revised Standard Version of the Bible: Catholic Edition*, copyright © 1965, 1966 the Division of Christian Education of the National Council of the Churches of Christ in the United States of America. Used by permission. All rights reserved.

The main content of this book was extracted from the book, *The Communal First Saturdays*, which received the *imprimatur* from His Eminence Daniel Cardinal DiNardo, the Archbishop of Galveston-Houston.

First Revised Edition July 13, 2022
105th Anniversary of Our Lady's 3rd Apparition at Fatima

Copyright © 2022 First Saturdays for Peace.
All rights reserved.

Email:
info@communalfirstsaturdays.org

www.CommunalFirstSaturdays.org

ISBN: 978-1-951233-04-4

In reparation for the sins committed against the Immaculate Heart of Mary

The Pilgrim Virgin Statue Church to Home Visitation

Contents

Introduction ix

The Pilgrim Virgin Statue Church to Home Visitation

Section One
The Order of Devotions for the Pilgrim Virgin Statue Church to Home Visitation

1. The Reception of the Pilgrim Virgin Statue in the Church 1
2. On Entering the Home 6
3. Recommendations for the Week-long Visit 11
4. The Enthronement of the Sacred Heart of Jesus, and the placement of the images of the Immaculate Heart of Mary and St. Joseph 13
5. The Return of the Pilgrim Virgin Statue to the Church 18

Section Two
Questions on the Meaning of the Pilgrim Virgin Statue Church to Home Visitation

1. *What is the Pilgrim Virgin Statue Church to Home Visitation?* 21
2. *What is the purpose of the Pilgrim Virgin Statue Church to Home Visitation?* 22
3. *What is the origin of the Pilgrim Virgin statue?* 25
4. *What does the Pilgrim Virgin statue have to do with the mystery of the Visitation?* 26
5. *What else can we learn from the mystery of the Visitation?* 26
6. *Is the mystery of the Visitation prefigured in the Old Testament?* 29
7. *Is there direct reference to the Ark of the Covenant in the New Testament?* 33
8. *Does the Ark of the Covenant prefigure anything else?* 34
9. *Does the Pilgrim Virgin statue represent anything else?* 40

10. Why would the Pilgrim Virgin statue go forth from and return to the First Saturday Masses and the other Saturday Masses? 40
11. Who brings the Pilgrim Virgin statue to the home or other venue? 41
12. Is it permitted to have more than one Pilgrim Virgin statue? 42
13. May a household receive the Pilgrim Virgin statue if there is already a statue of the Virgin Mary in the dwelling? 42
14. Is the Pilgrim Virgin statue necessary to the Communal First Saturdays? 42
15. Does the visit of the Pilgrim Virgin statue of Our Lady provide a form of outreach from the Communal First Saturdays? 43
16. Are there other ways that the Pilgrim Virgin statue visitation may be an apostolate of the Communal First Saturdays? 44
17. Why say the Rosary in the home, the church, or elsewhere? 46
18. Why is the body of the Rosary necessary if the soul of the prayer, the meditation, is more important? 49
19. Why should we meditate on the mysteries of the Rosary? 51
20. Why say the family Rosary? 52
21. What are the fifteen promises of the Rosary? 55
22. Is it possible to gain a plenary indulgence by praying the Rosary or in fulfilling the First Saturdays? 57

Section Three
Questions on the Enthronement of the Sacred Heart of Jesus and the Placement of the Images of the Immaculate Heart of Mary and St. Joseph

23. What is the enthronement of the Sacred Heart of Jesus? 61
24. Why does the visit of the Pilgrim Virgin statue culminate in the enthronement of the Sacred Heart of Jesus? 61
25. How do we prepare for the enthronement of the Sacred Heart of Jesus? 62
26. What are some of the promises of the Sacred Heart of Jesus to St. Margaret Mary? 64
27. May the enthronement be accompanied by the placement of an image of the Immaculate Heart of Mary in the home? 70
28. May the enthronement be accompanied by the placement of an image of St. Joseph in the home? 71

Contents

Appendix A
How to Say the Rosary

How to pray the Rosary 79

Appendix B
Information on the First Saturdays Devotion

1. What did Our Lady of the Rosary at Fatima say God wants? 85
2. What has been done? 85
3. Pope Benedict XVI's Words at Fatima 85
4. What is the Communion of reparation on the First Saturdays? (also known as the First Saturdays devotion) 85
5. What are the two promises made by Our Lady in regard to the First Saturdays? 86
6. Why are there 5 First Saturdays? 86
7. Why is it important to make reparation to the Immaculate Heart of Mary? 87
8. What if I start the First Saturdays one month and cannot complete it the next month? 87
9. What if I forget to do one of the practices of the five First Saturdays? 87
10. How do I keep Our Lady company for a quarter of an hour while meditating on the mysteries of the Rosary with the intention of making reparation to her Immaculate Heart? 88
11. Is it all right to meditate on any of the mysteries of the Rosary that one wishes? 88
12. What if I cannot go to Confession on the First Saturday? 88
13. Remember 88
14. Power in Prayer Together 89

Appendix C
Hymns

Hail, Holy Queen Enthroned Above 93
Immaculate Mary 93

Contact Information 95

Introduction

"And why is this granted me, that the mother of my Lord should come to me?" *(Lk. 1:43)*

What is the Pilgrim Virgin Statue Church to Home Visitation?

      The *Pilgrim Virgin Statue Church to Home Visitation* is designed to begin in the church after the *Communal First Saturdays* and the other Saturday Masses. This visitation is quite different from any other Pilgrim Virgin program. Instead of going from home to home, the Pilgrim Virgin statue travels from the parish church to the home or other venue following the Holy Mass with the purpose of bringing about the Enthronement of the Sacred Heart of Jesus in the home or other venue. The mission of the Pilgrim Virgin statue is then completed by returning with the family to the Mass on the following Saturday. Simply put, Our Lady always seeks to bring us to her Son.

What is the Communal First Saturdays?

      The *Communal First Saturdays* is a monthly **scheduled parish service** in which the faithful can **join together in the four practices** requested by Our Lady of Fatima (1925) **in reparation** to her Immaculate Heart. **Confessions** are available before Mass. The recitation of the **Rosary precedes Mass** which includes the **Communion of reparation**. The Mass is followed by keeping Our Lord and Our Lady company while **meditating communally for 15 minutes** on the mysteries of the Rosary. This is done in the form of *lectio divina* and using **Scripture** related to the mysteries of the Rosary. The reception of the Pilgrim Virgin statue follows. A book is used by the faithful to follow the service.

      The *Communal First Saturdays* makes it **easier** for each person and for a **larger number** of the faithful to fulfill the *First Saturdays* practices. For more information, please see the website listed below.

Why does Our Lady come from the Saturday Mass to the home?

      The journey from the church to the home is like Mary's journey from Nazareth to the town in Judah. Also, Jesus became incarnate within Mary before the journey to Judah, and He becomes present in the Eucharist which we can receive at Mass before the journey of the Pilgrim Virgin statue to the home. Further, in the Old Testament, God was present upon the Ark of the Covenant containing the manna, prefiguring the Holy Eucharist.

The Pilgrim Virgin Statue Church to Home Visitation

The Ark of the Covenant would also journey from place to place. Mary is called the Ark of the Covenant, and her Pilgrim Virgin statue reminds us of the way in which she fulfills the meaning of this title. In addition, the people are sent out at the end of Mass. The journey of the Pilgrim Virgin statue from the Mass is a symbol of this. Also, the Enthronement of the Sacred Heart of Jesus in the home helps lead the family back to the greatest gift of the Heart of Jesus which is the Holy Eucharist. For the devotions to the Sacred Heart of Jesus and the Holy Eucharist are inseparable.

The *Pilgrim Virgin Statue Church to Home Visitation* has a special connection with the *Communal First Saturdays*. **First,** Our Lady of Fatima's request for the *First Saturdays* took place at Pontevedra, Spain. This city is well known for the Pilgrim Virgin chapel which commemorates the appearance of Our Lady as a pilgrim accompanying the other pilgrims on the way through Pontevedra to Santiago de Compostela, which for centuries has been one of the most important destinations of all Catholic pilgrimages. **Second,** the action step of the meditation after the *Communal First Saturdays* Mass calls us to go with haste with Our Lady as represented by the Pilgrim Virgin statue. **Third,** the reception of the Pilgrim Virgin statue at the end of the *Communal First Saturdays* includes a reenactment of the mystery of Our Lady's visit to Elizabeth. **Fourth,** the Pilgrim Virgin statue goes to the home with the Fatima message which calls for the *First Saturdays*. **Fifth,** the *Pilgrim Virgin Statue Church to Home Visitation* is an extension of the *Communal First Saturdays* into the home for an entire week. **Sixth,** one of the five reasons given by Our Lord for the *First Saturdays* is the mistreatment of Our Lady's images. The devotion of the Pilgrim Virgin statue can help to make reparation for these sins. **Seventh,** the reception and return of the Pilgrim Virgin statue on other Saturdays provide an opportunity to invite the faithful to come to the *Communal First Saturdays*. Also, the faithful attending the *Communal First Saturdays* can be invited to have the Enthronement of the Sacred Heart of Jesus in their home through the visit of the Pilgrim Virgin statue.

Why would Our Lady want to visit me?

Everything begins with God. "God so loved the world that He sent His only begotten Son" (Jn. 3:16). In sending His Son, "God has visited and redeemed His people" (Lk. 1:68). We also read, "And the Word was made flesh, and dwelt among us" (Jn. 1:14). In this way, by becoming flesh in the womb of the Virgin Mary, He visited us and so manifested His love for us. After conceiving Jesus, Mary went with haste to visit a family in need (Lk. 1:39-56). In doing so she brought her Son as well. Thus, God Himself

Introduction

visited this family. In Our Lady's great love for us, she wishes to bring her Son to us. At the same time, Our Lady wishes to bring us to her Son. This is one of the reasons why Jesus wishes to bring His Mother to us and bring us to His Mother.

Let us recall the words spoken by Jesus as He hung upon the Cross. Before addressing St. John, Jesus first said to His Mother, "Woman, behold your son" (Jn. 19:26). This reference to "Woman" proclaims to the whole world that this is the woman referred to in the book of Genesis: "I will put enmity between you [Satan] and the woman" (3:15, brackets are ours). Satan and Our Lady are enemies. A war is being waged over souls. Satan seeks to tear us away from Jesus, and Our Lady seeks to bring us to Jesus. In addressing Our Lady first from the Cross, Jesus gave us to her as her children. As our spiritual Mother, she loves us all, and you in particular. We all need our Blessed Mother's love. Our very life depends upon it because all graces come from Jesus through Mary to us.

As a mother, Our Lady wishes to visit you. She who is "full of grace" wishes to be a channel of grace to you. Call to mind again the example Mary gave when she visited her kinswoman Elizabeth. Mary went to help Elizabeth who was with child. Our Lady was an instrument of many graces to this family, and in particular the grace of the mission of John the Baptist. Our Lady also has in mind special graces just for you and your family as she continues this mystery of the Visitation by the visit of her Pilgrim Virgin statue.

Why would I want Our Lady to visit me?

Jesus told us, "Enter by the narrow gate; for the gate is wide and the way is easy that leads to destruction" (Mt. 7:13). This life is like a drop in the ocean. It is over very quickly and then we begin our life in eternity which never ends. We need to enter through Jesus Who is the narrow gate, but how can we do this?

After addressing Mary, His Mother, beneath the Cross, Jesus looked at the disciple who represented all of us and said, "Behold your Mother!" (Jn. 19:27). In the person of the disciple, all people are being asked to recognize their Mother and to take her into their homes. "And from that hour the disciple took her into his home" (Jn. 19:27). Jesus wants us all to recognize His Mother through whom we receive our spiritual life. Jesus calls us to respond to Mary's maternal love for us. We must not turn away from so loving a mother who suffered so much for all of us beneath the Cross.

Yet, our Blessed Mother also suffered for us throughout her life so that we might have eternal life. We recall the words of Simeon to Mary when Joseph and she brought the Child Jesus to the temple to consecrate Him to the Lord: "A sword shall pierce your soul so that the hearts of many may be revealed" (Lk. 2:35). These words began to be fulfilled beneath the Cross, and experienced in Our Lady's own Heart when the lance pierced the side of the body of her Son. When we reflect on our Mother's suffering, what is revealed about our hearts, your heart? How much do we care about our Mother's suffering? Do we respond with compassion toward her? She is asking if she may visit you. Will you welcome her? Will you grant her this consolation? Will you, like John, take her into your own home? Recall that when the Ever-virgin Mary was about to miraculously deliver her Child in Bethlehem that Joseph and she were turned away. In turning Mary and Joseph away, they were turning Jesus away. "For there was no room for them at the inn" (Lk. 2:7). Will you make room for Them now? Caring about others is essential to our salvation so that we might enter through the narrow gate. In caring about Our Lady, we are already beginning to care about others. By caring for our spiritual Mother, we will better appreciate her care for us.

Why is the visit of the Blessed Mother important to my family?

Again, Our Lady leads us to her Son. Our Lady also leads us to one another. Our Lady begins to do this through her prayer to her Son, and our prayer to her. As Our Lady unites us with her Son, she also unites us with one another. "The family that prays together stays together." In this way, the family becomes what it is meant to be. The family becomes a community of love and life. The family begins to live as the domestic church. Yet, Mary is both the model and the Mother of the Church. Thus she is the model and the Mother of the family. Mary models a loving mother in the family. For instance, she sought to nurture her Child and provided for His needs. One of the needs Mary provided for was the education of her Son Jesus. In a similar manner, one's religious education should begin in the family (See *Catechism of the Catholic Church*, n. 2225-2226). Through the visit of the Pilgrim Virgin statue, the entire family can learn about the things of God.

Through the *Pilgrim Virgin Statue Church to Home Visitation*, the family is encouraged to walk in the way of the Gospel message, a message which unites the family in Faith, Hope, and Love. During Our Lady's visit, she invites us to join with her in praying the Rosary. The Rosary, the Gospel prayer, helps to anchor the family in the message of the Gospel and prepare

Introduction

it for Jesus in the Holy Eucharist. By praying the Rosary, the family becomes a community united in truth as well as in prayer.

How can our Blessed Mother visit me?

As mentioned above, our loving Mother wishes to visit us. On our part, this requires an act of Faith. We believe what we cannot see. If we believe that Our Lady is the best of mothers, and she is, then we realize that she wishes to visit us, to come to us. She wants to be with us. She wants to save us by leading us to Jesus. At the same time, we are human, body and soul. As human, it is our nature to rely on our senses. Jesus recognized this need to rely on our senses when He gave us the sacraments as sensible signs, which give us grace and lift up our minds to what we cannot see. (See *Catechism of the Catholic Church*, n. 1131). Seeing the Pilgrim Virgin statue come into our home reminds us of our Mother Mary who wishes to help us lift up our hearts to her Son.

So we wish to represent the visit of Our Lady by means of a statue. The statue that we receive is that of Our Lady of the Rosary who appeared at Fatima. Venerable Pope Pius XII sent out the first two international Pilgrim Virgin statues of Our Lady of Fatima (Our Lady of the Rosary) in 1947, and a large number of Pilgrim Virgin statues have been traveling from place to place ever since.

Our hope is that many parishes will send out Pilgrim Virgin statues to homes and other places from the *Communal First Saturdays* following the Mass and Scripture meditation, and following the Mass on other Saturdays as well. Immediately following the Mass and/or meditation, there would be a reception of the Pilgrim Virgin statue at the church. Included in the reception on *First Saturdays* are the readings regarding the mystery of the Visitation in the Gospel of St. Luke. The recipient(s) would then bring the Pilgrim Virgin statue home.

What does our Blessed Mother want to do when she comes to my home?

When Our Lady arrived at the house of Zechariah, Elizabeth became filled with the Holy Spirit at the sound of Mary's voice, and the child John the Baptist was sanctified in Elizabeth's womb (Lk. 1:15, 41). This sanctification included the special mission entrusted to John the Baptist to prepare the people for Jesus by repentance and to proclaim Jesus as the Lamb of God (Lk. 1:76-77, Jn. 1:29). Through the mission and ministry that John the Baptist received by Our Lady's visit, he was able to bring the most important Apostles to Jesus along with many others for the building up of the Church. In this way, Our Lady's humble visit to Elizabeth had an essential part in the formation of the Church.

In a similar fashion, in coming to the home from the Saturday Mass with the host family, Our Lady wishes to be a channel of the outpouring of the Holy Spirit into the hearts of all who receive her. Also, Our Lady wants to obtain a special grace for each one of her children's unique mission in life. This grace will help each one of us to carry out our own unique part in the plan of God.

It is also true that Our Lady wishes to bring the message of the Gospel into our homes through the message of Fatima. "If the Church has accepted the message of Fatima, it is above all because that message contains a truth and a call whose basic content is the truth and the call of the Gospel itself" (St. John Paul II, homily at Fatima, May 13, 1982). This is a message to be lived. The Holy Spirit wants to help us live this message and find joy in doing our part in sharing the word of God, so needed in our times.

Finally, Our Lady wishes to bring us to the Heart of her Son and her Son to us. She wishes to establish a permanent remembrance of the Sacred Heart of Jesus in our homes and a constant reminder that the home is the domestic church. Our Lady's visit culminates in returning us to the Mass that we might be united to her Son in the Holy Eucharist.

What do we do when our Blessed Mother visits our home?

When the Pilgrim Virgin statue enters the home for the week, it is recommended that one follow the format in this book. If possible, the family is encouraged to pray the Rosary daily. During the week, one is free to make use of the various materials that may be found in a carrying case that may accompany the Pilgrim Virgin statue. For example, one may find a Catholic Bible, the *Catechism of the Catholic Church*, and DVDs on the Fatima message, as well as other religious materials.

We have discussed in this writing that the Immaculate Heart of Mary wishes to prepare us for the Enthronement of the Sacred Heart of Jesus in a special place in the home. This devotion also includes the placement of the images of the Immaculate Heart of Mary and St. Joseph. The prayers for this devotion include the Rosary, acts of consecration to the Sacred Heart of Jesus and the Immaculate Heart of Mary, and an act of reparation to the Sacred Heart of Jesus. In these communal prayers we proclaim our home to be the domestic church.

Introduction

Finally, the most important purpose of Our Lady's visit is to bring the family back to the Holy Eucharist in the Mass on the following Saturday, and especially, the First Saturday.

How do I schedule a visit of the Pilgrim Virgin statue?

Please contact the *Pilgrim Virgin Statue Church to Home Visitation* coordinator for your parish.

(The above text can also be found in the "The Pilgrim Virgin Statue Church to Home Visitation" pamphlet, which can be found at www.CommunalFirstSaturdays.org).

Organization of this book

Section One of this book provides all that you need for the order of devotion for the *Pilgrim Virgin Statue Church to Home Visitation* on the First Saturdays in the church as well as on other Saturdays. This section also provides additional information on what is recommended to take place in the home while the Pilgrim Virgin Statue is there.

Section Two of this books provides answers to questions on the meaning of the *Pilgrim Virgin Statue Church to Home Visitation*. Section Three provides answers to questions on the Enthronement of the Sacred Heart of Jesus and the placement of the images of the Immaculate Heart of Mary and St. Joseph. Appendix A provides information on how to pray the Rosary, Appendix B provides information on the First Saturdays Devotion and Appendix C contains hymns that the family or individual can sing.

Section One

The Order of Devotions for the Pilgrim Virgin Statue Church to Home Visitation

1. The Reception of the Pilgrim Virgin Statue in the Church

With the additional approval of the pastor, a blessed Pilgrim Virgin statue of Our Lady is formally received by the host in the church following the Communal First Saturdays and possibly following the morning Mass on other Saturdays as well. This ensures a strong connection with the Communal First Saturdays and, most important, a strong connection between the Liturgy in the church and the home, the domestic church. If possible, the Pilgrim Virgin statue is placed in the sanctuary near the altar for the Saturday morning Mass.

(It is possible to have present several blessed Pilgrim Virgin statues to travel to other homes, nursing homes, and/or place(s) of Pro-Life apostolate. In addition, a blessed image(s) of Our Lady of Guadalupe could be made available for Pro-Life apostolate. It is suggested that these additional images of Our Lady ordinarily be covered during the reception so that one can focus on one image).

The reception of the Pilgrim Virgin statue on the First Saturdays

*The Pilgrim Virgin statue custodian (PVS custodian or other leader) would read the part of the **narrator**. The person reading the part of **Mary** (the person returning the statue that week if possible) and the person reading the part of **Elizabeth** (the person receiving the statue that week if possible) and their family members stand at the foot of the sanctuary. If there are other host(s) whether as individuals or families receiving a statue or other image, they should also stand at the foot of the sanctuary. It is recommended that these additional images be covered and carefully placed on a nearby table or in the first pew.*
The narrator also stands at the foot of the sanctuary.

***Narrator*:** Please turn to page 2 in your books to follow along.

The narrator says the following if there is more than one image of Our Lady present at the reception:

The Pilgrim Virgin Statue Church to Home Visitation

Narrator: (There is more than one image of Our Lady present at the reception this week. The additional image(s) will be covered so that our attention will be focused on one image.)

The following is said whether there are one or more images to be returned and/or received:

Narrator: We ask that anyone who is returning and/or receiving an image of Our Lady come to the foot of the sanctuary.

Narrator: Before we begin, let us try to think of the Pilgrim Virgin statue coming from the sanctuary to the foot of the sanctuary as representing Our Lady's journey from Nazareth to the house of Zechariah on a mission of mercy.

The narrator leads the person reading Mary's part from the foot of the sanctuary to the main Pilgrim Virgin statue in the sanctuary. Both bow to the Blessed Sacrament if present. The person reading the part of Elizabeth should stand near the foot of the sanctuary.
The narrator or an assistant would then present the Pilgrim Virgin statue to the person reading the part of Mary.

The narrator continues:

Narrator: "In those days Mary arose and went with haste into the hill country, to a city of Judah" *(Pause)*

After they both bow to the Blessed Sacrament (if present), the narrator then accompanies the person reading Mary's part to meet the person reading Elizabeth's part at the foot of the sanctuary. In doing so, the person reading Mary's part brings the Pilgrim Virgin statue to the foot of the sanctuary representing Mary's journey to the house of Zechariah.

Narrator: "…and she entered the house of Zechari'ah and greeted Elizabeth. And when Elizabeth heard the greeting of Mary, the child leaped in her

Section One

                womb; and Elizabeth was filled with the Holy Spirit and she exclaimed with a loud cry,

Elizabeth: 'Blessed are you among women, and blessed is the fruit of your womb! And why is this granted me, that the mother of my Lord should come to me? For behold, when the voice of your greeting came to my ears, the child in my womb leaped for joy. And blessed is she who believed that there would be a fulfilment of what was spoken to her from the Lord.'"

Narrator: "And Mary said:

Mary: 'My soul magnifies the Lord;
and my spirit rejoices in God my Savior,

All: for he has regarded the low estate of his handmaiden.
For behold, henceforth all generations will call me blessed;
for he who is mighty has done great things for me,
and holy is his name.
And his mercy is on those who fear him
from generation to generation.
He has shown strength with his arm,
he has scattered the proud in the imagination of their hearts,
he has put down the mighty from their thrones,
and exalted those of low degree;
he has filled the hungry with good things,
and the rich he has sent empty away.
He has helped his servant Israel,
in remembrance of his mercy,
as he spoke to our fathers,
to Abraham and to his posterity forever.'"

(Pause)

The narrator now addresses the person who reads the part of Mary:

The Pilgrim Virgin Statue Church to Home Visitation

Narrator: Please present the Pilgrim Virgin statue to the next host, _____(*name of host*).

The Pilgrim Virgin statue is presented to the new host.

As the Pilgrim Virgin statue(s) and/or image(s) is/are presented to the next host(s), the narrator says:

Narrator: Receive the Pilgrim Virgin statue. *(Pause)*

Narrator: "And Mary remained with her about three months, and returned to her home" *(Lk. 1:39-56). (Pause)*

Narrator: As Our Lady brought Jesus into the home of Elizabeth and Zechariah and by the Holy Spirit, Elizabeth acknowledged the real presence of Jesus in Mary, so now Our Lady wishes to bring the Sacred Heart of Jesus into our homes and then bring us back to the real presence of Jesus in the Mass.

Without words, any additional covered Pilgrim Virgin statues or images would be presented to the other new host(s) as well.

Narrator: Please turn your books to page 5 for the hymn, "Immaculate Mary." You may follow behind the procession if you wish.

After bowing in front of the Blessed Sacrament (if present), the narrator, new host(s) and any new host family members begin to process toward the narthex/vestibule.[1] The previous host(s) and any family members present proceed next, followed by the congregation.

---

[1] *The new host(s) would then place the statue(s) on a table. The PVS custodian would then 1) place the statue(s) in the protective carrier(s) and 2) before the carrier is closed, point out any helpful related materials, and 3) especially ask the host(s) to look at the rest of this book, so the host(s) can find information regarding what can take place in the home as well as read and develop an understanding of the meaning of the Pilgrim Virgin statue and the enthronement of the Sacred Heart of Jesus. (If the enthronement of the Sacred Heart of Jesus has already taken place, it is recommended that the enthronement be renewed with each visitation).*

Section One

While processing, all sing "Immaculate Mary" or other approved Marian hymn.

Immaculate Mary

All: Immaculate Mary, your praises we sing;
You reign now in splendor with Jesus our King.
Ave, ave, ave, Maria! Ave, ave, Maria!

In heaven, the blessed your glory proclaim;
On earth we, your children, invoke your sweet name.
Ave, ave, ave, Maria! Ave, ave, Maria!

We pray for the Church, our true Mother on earth,
And beg you to watch o'er the land of our birth.
Ave, ave, ave, Maria! Ave, ave, Maria!

After the procession comes to a halt in the designated place (such as the narthex/vestibule), the narrator could announce how one can schedule the "Pilgrim Virgin Statue Church to Home Visitation" and/or receive First Saturdays information. The following are examples of wording:

Narrator

- "For those of you who would like to open your homes to the *Pilgrim Virgin Statue Church to Home Visitation* for a week, you may sign up in the _____*(designated place such as the narthex/vestibule)."*
- "There is a pamphlet *(hold up "The Pilgrim Virgin Statue Church to Home Visitation" pamphlet)* that explains more about this as well as the enthronement of the Sacred Heart of Jesus that can take place in the home."
- "If you would like *First Saturdays* information and updates, there is also a 2nd sign up sheet for you to give your name and email."

Other applicable announcements and closing:

- *Announce where the Brown Scapular may be received.*

The Pilgrim Virgin Statue Church to Home Visitation

- *Announce where to return the books.*
- *Announce that the Pilgrim Virgin statue will now be prepared for transportation.*
- *Thank the faithful for coming and ask them to come again to the next Communal First Saturdays.*

The host then proceeds to the place where the image of Our Lady will remain for one week.

The reception of the Pilgrim Virgin statue on other Saturdays

After Mass, if applicable, after the priest has processed out, the Pilgrim Virgin statue (PVS) custodian would then 1) bring the protective carrier(s) with the statue(s) to a table in the designated place for the reception, 2) set the statue(s) on the table, and 3) place, as recommended, a cover on all statues except one. In the presence of the host receiving the statue the PVS custodian would then begin:

PVS custodian: In the Name of the Father and of the Son and of the Holy Spirit. Amen.

PVS custodian: Let us recall the following words from Scripture: "In those days Mary arose and went with haste into the hill country, to a city of Judah" *(Pause).*

PVS custodian: Receiving the Pilgrim Virgin statue symbolizes that we receive Our Lady who goes out from the Mass to bring the Sacred Heart of Jesus into our homes. *(Pause)*

PVS custodian: In the Name of the Father and of the Son and of the Holy Spirit. Amen.

2. On Entering the Home

Everything written in italics is intended for the guidance of the host and would not be read to those attending the visitation of the Pilgrim Virgin statue, or the enthronement of the Sacred Heart of Jesus in the home. Italics within a prayer would indicate an alternative word choice.

Section One

Through Faith we realize that our Blessed Mother wishes to come into our home. Our Lady comes with a Heart full of love for each one of us and she wishes that by the Holy Spirit our hearts may be joined ever more closely to the Sacred Heart of her Son. It is important to know that the purpose of the Pilgrim Virgin statue devotion is to lead us to the Eucharistic Heart of Jesus in the Mass. Our Lady brings the Fatima message into the home to lead us to the reign of the Sacred Heart of Jesus in the home, symbolized by the enthronement of the Sacred Heart of Jesus. The enthronement is the high point of Our Lady's visit in the home. The enthronement of the Sacred Heart of Jesus in the home should be a reminder to us that the Holy Eucharist is the greatest Gift of His love for us.

A special place should already be prepared for the statue of Our Lady before going to the church to receive the statue. This special place should also ordinarily be the place where the enthronement of the Sacred Heart of Jesus will occur later in the week. A cloth, candle(s), and flowers could be arranged for the statue if possible. On entering the home, the householder will place the statue in this special place.

On First Saturdays

On the First Saturdays, say the prayer to the Holy Spirit on page 9 and the Hail Mary. If the family was not present for the Rosary and other prayers before Mass, then the prayers on pages 9-11 may then be recited by all present at home. In any case, end with the "Daily Prayer in Preparation for the Enthronement of the Sacred Heart of Jesus" on page 11.

On Saturdays other than First Saturdays

Our Lady is welcomed in the home with the passages of the Scripture reading taken from the Gospel of St. Luke (1:39-56). These passages provide inspired material for the reenactment of Our Lady's visit to Elizabeth. If possible, the different parts can be taken by different persons present. The part of Elizabeth may be taken by the mother or daughter of the home. Alternatively, the Scripture verses may be read by one person. We recall that at the sound of Mary's voice Elizabeth was filled with the Holy Spirit. So may the prayer of Our Lady obtain that the Holy Spirit be poured out upon this home or apostolate.

Narrator: "In those days Mary arose and went with haste into the hill country, to a city of Judah"

The Pilgrim Virgin Statue Church to Home Visitation

All may sing the following hymn or the narrator continues.

Immaculate Mary

All: Immaculate Mary, your praises we sing;
You reign now in splendor with Jesus our King.
Ave, ave, ave, Maria! Ave, ave, Maria!

In heaven, the blessed your glory proclaim;
On earth we, your children, invoke your sweet name.
Ave, ave, ave, Maria! Ave, ave, Maria!

We pray for the Church, our true Mother on earth,
And beg you to watch o'er the land of our birth.
Ave, ave, ave, Maria! Ave, ave, Maria!

The narrator continues.

Narrator: "…and she entered the house of Zechari'ah and greeted Elizabeth. And when Elizabeth heard the greeting of Mary, the child leaped in her womb; and Elizabeth was filled with the Holy Spirit and she exclaimed with a loud cry,

Elizabeth: 'Blessed are you among women, and blessed is the fruit of your womb! And why is this granted me, that the mother of my Lord should come to me? For behold, when the voice of your greeting came to my ears, the child in my womb leaped for joy. And blessed is she who believed that there would be a fulfilment of what was spoken to her from the Lord.'"

Narrator: "And Mary said:

Mary: 'My soul magnifies the Lord;
and my spirit rejoices in God my Savior,

All: for he has regarded the low estate of his handmaiden.
For behold, henceforth all generations will call

Section One

        me blessed;
        for he who is mighty has done great things for me,
        and holy is his name.
        And his mercy is on those who fear him
        from generation to generation.
        He has shown strength with his arm,
        he has scattered the proud in the imagination of their hearts,
        he has put down the mighty from their thrones,
        and exalted those of low degree;
        he has filled the hungry with good things,
        and the rich he has sent empty away.
        He has helped his servant Israel,
        in remembrance of his mercy,
        as he spoke to our fathers,
        to Abraham and to his posterity forever.'"

Narrator: "And Mary remained with her about three months, and returned to her home" *(Lk. 1:39-56). (Pause)*

After the above Scripture reading, the family may continue with the following prayers.

Intention to gain any indulgences

For more information on indulgences, see q. 22 in Section Two.

Leader: Let us make the intention to gain any indulgences granted by the Church for ourselves and the souls in Purgatory.

Come Holy Spirit

Come, Holy Spirit, fill the hearts of your faithful and enkindle in them the fire of your love.

V. Send forth your Spirit, and they shall be created.
R. And You shall renew the face of the earth.

Let us pray.

O God, Who by the light of the Holy Spirit did instruct the hearts of the faithful, grant that in the same Spirit, we may be truly wise, and ever rejoice in His consolation. Through Christ Our Lord. Amen.

The Rosary

If the Rosary has not already been said before the Saturday Mass or otherwise that day, it is recommended that the Rosary be recited as an excellent way to welcome Our Blessed Mother into the home (or place of apostolate). See Appendix A, "How to Pray the Rosary."

The mysteries chosen on Saturdays are ordinarily the Joyful mysteries.

Prayers for the intentions of the Holy Father

Following the Rosary, prayers for the intentions of the Holy Father are recommended. These prayers will satisfy for one of the conditions to gain a plenary indulgence (see q. 22 in Section Two for more information).

Leader: Let us pray for the intentions of the Holy Father.

All: Our Father...
Hail Mary...
Glory Be...

Act of Consecration to the Immaculate Heart of Mary

All:

Heavenly Father, You so loved us that you sent Your only begotten Son Who emptied Himself, taking the form of a slave in the womb of the Blessed Virgin Mary by the power of the Holy Spirit for our salvation. Grant that as Jesus made a total Gift of Himself in His Sacrifice on the Cross, we may make a total return of ourselves to You through the Sacred Heart of Your Son and with the intercession of the Immaculate Heart of Mary.

Loving Jesus, grant that we may renew our personal consecration to You this day, a consecration that began with our Baptism. By that same Baptism, we acknowledge that we are totally yours and all we have is yours. Help us, loving Savior, to renew our baptismal promises to reject Satan, to reject sin, and to profess the Catholic Faith no matter what the cost. May we serve you by our baptismal anointing as priest, prophet, and king through the intercession of the Maternal Heart of Your Mother. You have given her to us as our own that we may offer to You a perfect and Immaculate Heart.

Loving Mother, we entrust to your Immaculate Heart our entire being, body and soul, and all that we have internal and external. Through your Maternal mediation and by the grace of the Holy Spirit, join us to the Heart of your Son, so that through Him we may come to the Father.

Loving Mother, grant that we may now return your love by offering reparation for the many sins that offend your Immaculate Heart. Grant that we may also fulfill your request for the *First Saturdays*. In this way, we hope, by the grace of the Holy Spirit, to obtain world peace and the salvation of souls, including our own. Amen.

Daily Prayer in Preparation for the Enthronement of the Sacred Heart of Jesus

All:

Merciful Father, draw us to the Heart of Your Son through the intercession of the Immaculate Heart of Mary. For no one comes to the Father except through Jesus. Prepare our hearts for the enthronement of the Sacred Heart of Jesus in our home, the domestic church (*other venue*). Father, grant that when we gaze upon the image of the Sacred Heart of Jesus, our hearts may be lifted up to contemplate Your immense love for us as well as His sacrificial love in giving His life for us. Grant that we may enthrone the Sacred Heart of Jesus in our home, the domestic church (*other venue*), as He was enthroned in the Heart of Mary. Grant that Your Son may be enthroned in our hearts as our King and Friend, knowing that where He is, so You Father also are there with the Holy Spirit. Grant that our hearts may always be gratefully united to the Immaculate Heart of Mary, our Mother, and that she may always lead us with gratitude to the Sacred Heart of Jesus, especially in the Holy Eucharist, the greatest Gift of His Heart. Amen.

3. Recommendations for the Week-long Visit

It is recommended that the Rosary and the prayers below be prayed as a family (or household or apostolate) each day or night before the Pilgrim Virgin statue of Our Lady (cf. Section Two, q. 17-21 on the Rosary;

The Pilgrim Virgin Statue Church to Home Visitation

also, in preparation for the enthronement, one may read Section Three, q. 23-28.

It is also recommended that the household or apostolate avail themselves of the parish-approved contents accompanying the Pilgrim Virgin statue such as the Bible, the Compendium of the Catechism of the Catholic Church, other literature, rosaries, scapulars, and DVDs concerning the Fatima message, as possible. Articles that must be returned with the statue may be labeled as such.

Intention to gain any indulgences

For more information on indulgences, please see q. 22 in Section Two.

Leader: Let us make the intention to gain any indulgences granted by the Church for ourselves and the souls in Purgatory.

The Rosary

The mysteries chosen may correspond to the day of the week. Ordinarily, the mysteries that may be chosen are as follows:

- *The Joyful mysteries on Mondays and Saturdays.*
- *The Luminous mysteries on Thursdays.*
- *The Sorrowful mysteries on Tuesdays and Fridays.*
- *The Glorious mysteries on Wednesdays and Sundays.*

The Rosary prayers may be found in Appendix A or in Rosary leaflets accompanying the Pilgrim Virgin statue (www.Rosary-center.org).

Prayers for the intentions of the Holy Father

Following the Rosary, prayers for the intentions of the Holy Father are recommended. These prayers will satisfy for one of the conditions to gain a plenary indulgence (see q.22 in Section Two).

Leader: Let us pray for the intentions of the Holy Father.

All: Our Father…
Hail Mary…
Glory Be…

Section One

Daily Prayer in Preparation for the Enthronement of the Sacred Heart of Jesus

All:
Merciful Father, draw us to the Heart of Your Son through the intercession of the Immaculate Heart of Mary. For no one comes to the Father except through Jesus. Prepare our hearts for the enthronement of the Sacred Heart of Jesus in our home, the domestic church (*other venue*). Father, grant that when we gaze upon the image of the Sacred Heart of Jesus, our hearts may be lifted up to contemplate Your immense love for us as well as His sacrificial love in giving His life for us. Grant that we may enthrone the Sacred Heart of Jesus in our home, the domestic church (*other venue*), as He was enthroned in the Heart of Mary. Grant that Your Son may be enthroned in our hearts as our King and Friend, knowing that where He is, so You Father also are there with the Holy Spirit. Grant that our hearts may always be gratefully united to the Immaculate Heart of Mary, our Mother, and that she may always lead us with gratitude to the Sacred Heart of Jesus, especially in the Holy Eucharist, the greatest Gift of His Heart. Amen.

4. The Enthronement of the Sacred Heart of Jesus, and the placement of the images of the Immaculate Heart of Mary and St. Joseph

One should read q. 23-28 in Section Three, "Questions on the Enthronement of the Sacred Heart of Jesus, and the Placement of the Images of the Immaculate Heart of Mary and St. Joseph." The image(s) could be provided with the Pilgrim Virgin statue and can already be blessed by a priest prior to the enthronement ceremony, unless a priest is to be present for the blessing of the image(s). If preferred, the host may later replace the images with other blessed images of the Sacred Heart of Jesus, the Immaculate Heart of Mary and St. Joseph

The enthronement may take place on the following Friday night or some other evening if necessary. One may invite friends, neighbors, and relatives to participate. The following prayers would begin as soon as the guests have arrived.

If the enthronement has already taken place *on a previous occasion, the household may say the following prayers and also* **renew the enthronement.**

Intention to gain any indulgences

The Pilgrim Virgin Statue Church to Home Visitation

For more information on indulgences, please see Section Two, q. 22.

Leader: Let us make the intention to gain any indulgences granted by the Church for ourselves and the souls in Purgatory.

The Rosary

The Rosary prayers may be found in Appendix A or in Rosary leaflets accompanying the Pilgrim Virgin statue (www.Rosary-center.org).

Prayers for the intentions of the Holy Father

Following the Rosary, prayers for the intentions of the Holy Father are recommended. These prayers will satisfy for one of the conditions to gain a plenary indulgence (see q. 22 in Section Two for more information).

Leader: Let us pray for the intentions of the Holy Father.

All: Our Father...
Hail Mary...
Glory Be...

Enthronement of the Sacred Heart of Jesus

The Pilgrim Virgin statue custodian could make available pictures of the Sacred Heart of Jesus, the Immaculate Heart of Mary, and St. Joseph for the enthronement and placement of images, respectively. The pictures or other images may be placed on a table from which they may be brought up to the place where the Sacred Heart of Jesus will be enthroned. If the pictures are to be hung on the wall, the proper hangars should already be in place. The picture or image of the Sacred Heart of Jesus would be brought first to the place where it will be placed or hung by the head of the household or another member of the family. Then the Sacred Heart of Jesus would be enthroned and all kneel if possible. The act of consecration and act of reparation to the Sacred Heart of Jesus would then follow.

Act of Consecration to the Sacred Heart of Jesus

All:

Section One

O Sacred Heart of Jesus Your love for us has no bounds. May we always be receptive to your infinite Mercy. O Sacred Heart of Jesus we offer You ourselves and our family *[household (or other)]*. We are totally Yours and all we have is Yours. O Sacred Heart of Jesus we offer everything to You through the Immaculate Heart of Mary. Reign in our hearts and reign in our home! We offer ourselves that we may be emptied out of ourselves. We empty ourselves that You may fill our emptiness with your infinite Love. May this household be united in Your Love, a Love that is pure and humble, a Love that is gentle and patient. Please sanctify this home with Your loving presence. May You, O Lord Jesus, ever see in us the Immaculate Heart of Your Mother instead of our own hearts, so that we may always receive You with gratitude and in a way that You deserve. May Your image in our home ever remind us that this household is consecrated to You as the domestic church in which You reign.

For a shorter form of the following prayer, the faithful may omit the parts in brackets.

Act of Reparation to the Sacred Heart of Jesus by Pope Pius XI

All:

O sweetest Jesus, whose overflowing charity towards men is most ungratefully repaid by such great forgetfulness, neglect and contempt, see, prostrate before Thy altars, we strive by special honor to make amends for the wicked coldness of men and the contumely with which Thy most loving Heart is everywhere treated.

At the same time, mindful of the fact that we too have sometimes not been free from unworthiness, and moved therefore with most vehement sorrow, in the first place we implore Thy mercy on us, being prepared by voluntary expiation to make amends for the sins we have ourselves committed, and also for the sins of those who wander far from the way of salvation, whether because, being obstinate in their unbelief, they refuse to follow Thee as their shepherd and leader, or because, spurning the vows of their Baptism, they have cast off the most sweet yoke of Thy law.

We now endeavor to expiate all these lamentable crimes together, and it is also our purpose to make amends for each one of them severally: for the want of modesty in life and dress, for impurities, for so many snares set for the minds of the innocent, for the violation of feast days, for the horrid blasphemies against Thee and Thy saints, for the insults offered to Thy Vicar and to the priestly order, for the neglect of the Sacrament of

Divine love or its profanation by horrible sacrileges, and lastly for the public sins of nations which resist the rights and the teaching authority of the Church which Thou hast instituted.

[Would that we could wash away these crimes with our own blood! And now, to make amends for the outrage offered to the Divine honor, we offer to Thee the same satisfaction which Thou didst once offer to Thy Father on the Cross and which Thou dost continually renew on our altars, we offer this conjoined with the expiations of the Virgin Mother and of all the Saints, and of all pious Christians, promising from our heart that so far as in us lies, with the help of Thy grace, we will make amends for our own past sins, and for the sins of others, and for the neglect of Thy boundless love, by firm faith, by a pure way of life, and by a perfect observance of the Gospel law, especially that of charity; we will also strive with all our strength to prevent injuries being offered to Thee, and gather as many as we can to become Thy followers.

Receive, we beseech Thee, O most benign Jesus, by the intercession of the Blessed Virgin Mary, the Reparatress, the voluntary homage of this expiation, and vouchsafe, by that great gift of final perseverance, to keep us most faithful until death in our duty and in Thy service, so that at length we may all come to that fatherland, where Thou with the Father and the Holy Ghost livest and reignest God for ever and ever.] Amen (*Miserentissimus Redemptor*, 1928).

The placement of the image of the Immaculate Heart of Mary

All Stand. The image of the Immaculate Heart of Mary is now brought forward and placed near the image of the Sacred Heart of Jesus. All kneel if possible. Then all continue with the act of consecration to the Immaculate Heart of Mary.

Act of Consecration to the Immaculate Heart of Mary

All:
Heavenly Father, You so loved us that you sent Your only begotten Son Who emptied Himself, taking the form of a slave in the womb of the Blessed Virgin Mary by the power of the Holy Spirit for our salvation. Grant that as Jesus made a total Gift of Himself in His Sacrifice on the Cross, we may make a total return of ourselves to You through the Sacred Heart of Your Son and with the intercession of the Immaculate Heart of Mary.

Section One

Loving Jesus, grant that we may renew our personal consecration to You this day, a consecration that began with our Baptism. By that same Baptism, we acknowledge that we are totally yours and all we have is yours. Help us, loving Savior, to renew our baptismal promises to reject Satan, to reject sin, and to profess the Catholic Faith no matter what the cost. May we serve you by our baptismal anointing as priest, prophet, and king through the intercession of the Maternal Heart of Your Mother. You have given her to us as our own that we may offer to You a perfect and Immaculate Heart.

Loving Mother, we entrust to your Immaculate Heart our entire being, body and soul, and all that we have internal and external. Through your Maternal mediation and by the grace of the Holy Spirit, join us to the Heart of your Son, so that through Him we may come to the Father.

Loving Mother, grant that we may now return your love by offering reparation for the many sins that offend your Immaculate Heart. Grant that we may also fulfill your request for the *First Saturdays*. In this way, we hope, by the grace of the Holy Spirit, to obtain world peace and the salvation of souls, including our own. Amen.

The placement of the image of St. Joseph

All stand. It is recommended that one place the image of St. Joseph alongside the images of Jesus and Mary. Should not the Holy Family be present in the home as the model of family life? Whether or not an image of St. Joseph is available, the prayer to St. Joseph may be said.

For a shorter form of the following prayer, the faithful may omit the part in brackets. All kneel if possible.

Prayer to St. Joseph

All:
Hail Joseph, shadow of the Father, guardian of the Redeemer, and protector of the way that leads to and through the Immaculate Heart of Mary, your true spouse. Please ask the Father to give us efficacious graces through the Heart of Jesus and by the Holy Spirit. Obtain by the intercession of the Heart of Mary that we faithfully fulfill Jesus and Mary's requests. Please present our offerings to and through the Immaculate Heart of Mary in reparation for the sins which have offended her and her Son. [Inspire us to fulfill and spread the *First Saturdays* and the Pilgrim Virgin statue visitation everywhere, so that many souls will be rescued from sin and be brought to

The Pilgrim Virgin Statue Church to Home Visitation

eternal life. Grant also as you blessed the world at Fatima with the Child Jesus, the Lamb of God, you bless us, and help us to build and maintain the civilization of love and peace which Our Lady has promised as the victory of her Immaculate Heart. For you are "...the faithful and wise servant, whom his master has set over his household, to give them their food at the proper time..." He set you "over all his possessions" (Mt. 24:45, 47). Thus we too wish to be entrusted entirely to your care, as members of your household for the honor and glory of the Hearts of Jesus and Mary.] Amen.

Sign the certificate of enthronement

The certificate of enthronement bears witness that the member(s) of this _____ (family, household, apostolate etc.), on a particular day, enthroned the Sacred Heart of Jesus in their _____(homes or other place). The certificate may be framed and hung beneath the enthroned image of the Sacred Heart of Jesus or at some other suitable place.

5. The Return of the Pilgrim Virgin Statue to the Church

After the week-long visit, the Pilgrim Virgin statue(s) should be returned to the church before Mass on Saturday. This signifies that Our Lady is leading us to her Son in the Holy Eucharist. It is recommended that those returning the Pilgrim Virgin statue(s) remain for the Holy Mass. Those who return the statue on a First Saturday are also asked to participate in the Communal First Saturdays, including the reception of the Pilgrim Virgin statue(s) by the next host(s) (cf. Reception of the Pilgrim Virgin statue on the First Saturdays above).

The Pilgrim Virgin statue custodian (PVS custodian) greets the host(s) returning the Pilgrim Virgin statue(s). The host(s) returning the Pilgrim Virgin statue(s) would present the statue(s) to the PVS custodian at the designated area. The PVS custodian would then place one statue on a nearby table. The PVS custodian would then say the following:

PVS custodian: In the Name of the Father and of the Son and of the Holy Spirit. Amen.

Welcome Blessed Mother and your children (*or child*)! For you, Mary, carried our Savior in your womb. "Blessed are you among women, and blessed is the fruit of your womb." *(Pause)* Let us call to mind that returning the Pilgrim Virgin statue before Mass symbolizes Our Lady bringing

Section One

the faithful to the Eucharistic Heart of Jesus present in the Mass.

(Pause)

PVS custodian: Our Lady visited your home to bring you to the Heart of her Son Jesus and brought you back to the church to be more closely united with His Eucharistic Heart. Our Lady has obtained many other blessings for you. Our Lady has consoled you by her Maternal love for you.

Is there anything we can do for Our Lady in return?
(Pause) Jesus has asked us to console Him and His Mother for the sins that offend them at every moment. Our Lord and His Mother have asked us to do this by trying to make reparation to her Immaculate Heart for the sins that have pierced her Heart. Our Lord and Our Lady have asked us to try to make reparation to her Immaculate Heart in a special way by making the *First Saturdays*.

The *Communal First Saturdays* here at (*name of parish or community*) will make this easier to do. You can be sure that in fulfilling the *First Saturdays*, there will be even greater blessings upon you and your family.

Then the PVS custodian could present to the returning host(s) a printed invitation to the next Communal First Saturdays together with an informational pamphlet on the Communal First Saturdays (pamphlet found at www.CommunalFirstSaturdays.org).

One uncovered Pilgrim Virgin statue would then be temporarily displayed in the designated area. If there is more than one Pilgrim Virgin statue, it is recommended that only one of the statues be uncovered so that the faithful can focus on one image.

Section Two

Questions on the Meaning of the Pilgrim Virgin Statue Church to Home Visitation

1. What is the Pilgrim Virgin Statue Church to Home Visitation?

The Pilgrim Virgin statue is an image which represents the Blessed Virgin Mary. This particular statue is often referred to as Our Lady of Fatima. It is important to remember though that when Our Lady appeared at Fatima, she identified herself as "the Lady of the Rosary." In doing so, she immediately added, "continue to say the Rosary every day."

What does it mean to call Our Lady of the Rosary a pilgrim? A pilgrim is one who travels about. A pilgrim may also be one who travels to a shrine or holy place as a religious act. This is what the Pilgrim Virgin statue does by visiting churches or homes and other places. International statues of Our Lady of Fatima travel from country to country. National Pilgrim Virgin statues travel from diocese to diocese within the same country. There are also various home visitation devotions which bring the Pilgrim Virgin statue from one home to another with the purpose of bringing the Gospel message of Fatima into the home. To a lesser extent there are home visitation devotions of the Pilgrim Virgin statue which offer the Enthronement of the Sacred Heart of Jesus.

The Pilgrim Virgin Statue Church to Home Visitation presented here with the *Communal First Saturdays* is quite different than any of the above. Instead of going from home to home, the Pilgrim statue travels from the parish church to the home or other venue following the Holy Mass with the purpose of bringing about the Enthronement of the Sacred Heart of Jesus. Simply put, Our Lady always seeks to bring us to her Son. Certainly, Our Lady brings the Fatima message into the home, but this Gospel message is itself a means to join us to the Sacred Heart of Jesus. The Enthronement of the Sacred Heart of Jesus acknowledges that we live in the presence of His love for us and that He is first in our lives. The image of the Sacred Heart enthroned reminds us that He is the Head and we are the members of His Body, the Church. In particular, the place of enthronement could be a place where the family can gather each day in communal prayer. This gathering reminds us that the Christian family is the domestic church.

Yet, there is more. Devotion to the Sacred Heart of Jesus is a devotion to the Holy Eucharist, which is the greatest Gift of His love for us. The Holy Eucharist is ordinarily celebrated in a church or chapel. It is fitting then that Our Lady by means of the Pilgrim Virgin statue comes forth from the church or chapel after the Holy Mass to establish the reign of the Sacred

The Pilgrim Virgin Statue Church to Home Visitation

Heart of Jesus in the home or other venue. After the week-long visit, the Pilgrim Virgin statue is then accompanied by the host(s) back to Holy Mass in the church since the fulfillment of the devotion to the Sacred Heart of Jesus is in the Holy Mass.

Yet, let us try to go a little more deeply into the journey of the Pilgrim Virgin statue from the church to the home (or other venue). In the *Communal First Saturdays* Mass or other Saturday Mass, as in any Mass, one can receive Jesus Who is then just as present within us as He was when Mary conceived Him at the Annunciation of the Angel. Having conceived Jesus, Mary then traveled to the home of Zechariah, Elizabeth, and John the Baptist. In that home, the family was filled with the Holy Spirit and Jesus was recognized. In like manner, following the Mass, having received Jesus, the host(s) travels with the Pilgrim Virgin statue to the home. In this way, Our Lady travels to a home with the mission of establishing devotion to the Sacred Heart of Jesus. By the enthronement of the Sacred Heart of Jesus, we are able to give further witness to our recognition of Jesus as King and Head of the home. After the week-long visit, Our Lady returns with the household to Jesus in His Body, Blood, Soul, and Divinity which becomes truly present in the Holy Mass. In the Holy Mass, the greatest Gift of Jesus' love, we can fully practice devotion to the Sacred Heart of Jesus. As a result, the meaning of the enthronement of the Sacred Heart of Jesus in the home is fulfilled in the Holy Mass which is the "source and summit" of our lives. The enthronement should remind us that the Mass comes forth from the Sacred Heart of Jesus. The return of the Pilgrim Virgin statue to the Holy Mass is the most important part of Our Lady's visit. The return of the Pilgrim Virgin statue to the church could occur every Saturday. Then, after the Holy Mass, the Pilgrim Virgin statue travels to another home or venue on the same day.

2. What is the purpose of the Pilgrim Virgin Statue Church to Home Visitation?

The special purpose of the *Pilgrim Virgin Statue Church to Home Visitation* is union with the Holy Eucharist, the greatest Gift of Jesus' love. Our Lady helps to achieve this purpose by bringing the Sacred Heart of Jesus devotion to the home by means of this visitation. The Pilgrim Virgin statue proceeds from the Holy Mass in church with the host and finally returns with the host to Jesus' real presence in the Holy Mass. Before the return of the Pilgrim Virgin statue to the church, and toward the end of Our Lady's visit, the Sacred Heart of Jesus is enthroned in the home. Enthroning the Sacred Heart of Jesus in the home provides a permanent reminder of His love, especially in the Gift of the Holy Eucharist. If the enthronement has already taken place, the enthronement is renewed during the visit of the Pilgrim Virgin statue. During the enthronement, acts of consecration and reparation are made to the Sacred Heart of Jesus. By the enthronement and prayers, we also encourage the family to truly be a domestic church.

One may read later in this book about the many blessings that the enthronement brings to the home and its members (cf. Section Three, q. 23-28). In the book, *The Communal First Saturdays*, we explain the even greater blessings of the Holy Eucharist (cf. Part II, Section One, Ch. 1, q. 9).

At the end of the week-long visit, the host and as many members of the family as possible accompany the Pilgrim Virgin statue back to the church. This symbolizes Our Lady bringing us to the Eucharistic Heart of Jesus in the church, and especially in the Mass. Here again, just as in the *Communal First Saturdays* and taught by the Magisterium, a devotion is ordered to the Liturgy (cf. *Marialis Cultus*, n. 31). Thus, both devotions, the *Communal First Saturdays* and the *Pilgrim Virgin Statue Church to Home Visitation*, lead the faithful to the Eucharistic Heart of Jesus in the Mass.

To help join us more closely to the Sacred Heart of Jesus, Our Lady also brings the Fatima message and with it many blessings into the home. Many Popes have called the Fatima message an affirmation of the Gospel, and a message for the whole world to hear. It serves as an excellent protection against the many false versions of the Gospel present in the world. The Fatima message not only calls for prayer and sacrifice, but asks for devotion to the Immaculate Heart of Mary. This devotion to the Immaculate Heart of Mary includes consecration and reparation. Thus, after the enthronement, an image of the Immaculate Heart of Mary is placed near the image of the Sacred Heart of Jesus. This is followed by acts of consecration and reparation to the Immaculate Heart of Mary. The image of the Immaculate Heart of Mary should remind us to be receptive to Jesus and to love Him in return. By the graces obtained through the Immaculate Heart of Mary, she lovingly continues to lead us to Jesus.

Upon returning the Pilgrim Virgin statue to the church, one might ask what can be done in return for the love our Blessed Mother showed us through her visit? One important way to respond to Our Lady's love is by fulfilling her special request for the *First Saturdays* of reparation and extending the spirituality of the *First Saturdays* into one's daily life. In this way, the *Pilgrim Virgin Statue Church to Home Visitation* not only acts as a form of outreach and mercy from the Mass, especially the *Communal First Saturdays* Mass, but also is an opportunity to invite the hosts to participate in the reparational devotion.

Participating in the *Communal First Saturdays* is an excellent way to fulfill Our Lady's request and support our daily practice of the Fatima message, since joining with others gives added strength and merit to our efforts. It is also often easier to fulfill Our Lady's request together with others (cf. *The Communal First Saturdays* book, Part II, Section Two, Ch. 4, q. 75, q. 76). At the same time, in addition to the four practices of the *First Saturdays*, other practices from the Fatima message are included in the *Communal First Saturdays* (cf. *The Communal First Saturdays Devotional* book, Fatima Prayers, Part I, 2.23 and Reception of the Brown Scapular, 2.27).

The Fatima message and the meaning of its practices can help to give us a deeper insight into our Faith. This message is not intended to take the place of the teachings of the Catholic Church, but the message does provide a great help for following Christ and understanding His teachings as taught by the Church.

We should keep in mind that the Fatima message is not meant to add something new to God's Revelation (the *Deposit of Faith*). Rather, through the Fatima message, God is simply making us more aware of the contents of His Revelation which was transmitted to the Apostles and by them to the rest of the Church. Also, by the Fatima message, God is highlighting those things in the Gospel which are needed in our time but may be neglected. In any case, we ourselves never come to the end of grasping what God has revealed.

Those who receive Our Lady with love will come to realize that she cannot be outdone in generosity, and will experience the outpouring of her maternal love. This maternal love leads us to the very Heart of her Son who wishes to be invited into our homes. In the Liturgy for the Mass on the feast of St. Martha, the Church prays, "Almighty ever living God, Whose Son was pleased to be welcomed in Saint Martha's house as a guest…." Like St. Martha, may we invite Jesus into our homes, and may we also invite His Mother to bring Him.

Through the help of the enthronement of His Sacred Heart, may Jesus come to stay permanently in our hearts and within our homes. We hope that Our Lady's visit and her Son's enthronement in our homes will help bring about an increase in holiness and the salvation of all touched by her visit. A true devotion to the Sacred Heart of Jesus can only mean a greater devotion to the greatest Gift of His love, the Holy Eucharist. An important added benefit of Our Lady's visit is the wonderful opportunity for the re-evangelization of the family. One of the most important ways that Our Lady does this is that she helps strengthen the inseparable link between the Christian home and the Liturgy. The practice of the *Communal First Saturdays* by the family can only help to further strengthen this bond rooted in the Sacrament of Baptism.

Section Two

3. What is the origin of the Pilgrim Virgin statue?

This practice of the Pilgrim Virgin statue visitation had its early beginnings when Venerable Pius XII authorized two international Pilgrim Statues to go forth from Fatima in 1946, one for the west and the other for the east. Venerable Pius XII recalled crowning the first international Pilgrim Virgin statue on May 13, 1951 in a radio address:

> In 1946 we crowned Our Lady of Fatima as Queen of the world, and the next year, through her pilgrim image, She set forth as though to claim Her dominion, and the miracles She performs along the way are such that we can scarcely believe our eyes at what we are seeing.

One of these international Pilgrim Virgin Statues finally entered Russia and Red Square in 1992 with 940 pilgrims having first flown above the Kremlin. Some thought this to have fulfilled a prophecy of St. Maximilian Kolbe that one day Our Lady would be seen above the Kremlin (cf. Di Lillo, *Incontri con Padre Massimiliano,* cit., pp. 64-65). In any case, a multitude of Pilgrim Virgin statues were sent out following the initial sending of the international statues in 1946. Seventy national statues were blessed and donated by the Bishop of Leiria-Fatima. Statues that could go to homes also began to be sent out.

Yet the inspiration for these statues goes back much earlier. One of the most ancient of Catholic pilgrimages is to the shrine of St. James the Greater, Santiago de Compestela in Spain. It is said that on one occasion the Virgin Mary appeared among the pilgrims on the way that leads through Pontevedra, Spain. In the 19th century, a chapel was built in Pontevedra called the Pilgrim Virgin Chapel to commemorate this occurrence. Yet there is more. It is here in Pontevedra that Fatima and the Pilgrim Virgin connect. This is so because it is Our Lady of Fatima who appeared to Sr. Lucia at her convent in Pontevedra on December 10th, 1925, together with the Child Jesus, to ask for the practice of the *First Saturdays*. In addition, Our Lady thereby associates the *First Saturdays* with herself as the Pilgrim Virgin, already honored by the Pilgrim Virgin Chapel also in Pontevedra, and for which the city is known. Thus, it is fitting that the Pilgrim Virgin statue(s) should go forth, especially from the *First Saturdays* Mass and, if possible, from all Saturday celebrations of the Mass. In this way, Our Lady may bless the home, the sick or elderly, and those with child.

The Pilgrim Virgin Statue Church to Home Visitation

In regard to the Pilgrim Virgin statue, a conversation between Lucia and the Archbishop of Cizico is worth mentioning:

> "Do you know, Sister, the meaning of those litters [carriers that can hold a statue or other objects with one or two persons at each end], which Our Lady told you to have made with the gifts that the people used to leave in the Cova da Iria? They were a prophecy of the litters used for the Pilgrim Virgin as she goes around the world, and the litter for the statue in the Chapel of Apparitions." I [Lucia] entirely agree with this interpretation because, in the mind of God, the same fact can have various meanings, and these journeys of Our Lady's image are yet another facet of the apostolate of the Message which she came to earth to bring, and which is traveling all over the world in search of people to bring them to God" *("CALLS" From the Message of Fatima*, Sister Lucia, trans. Sisters of Mosteiro de Santa Maria and Conventu de N.S. de Bom Succeso, Lisbon, p. 149, brackets are ours).

4. What does the Pilgrim Virgin statue have to do with the Mystery of the Visitation?

It is easy to see that the reception of the Pilgrim Virgin statue in the church and the week-long visit in the home reenact the mystery of the Visitation, and one could say even perpetuate that mystery by the visit of Our Lady to the homes of her children. Our Lady wishes to bring great blessings upon the home as she did when she visited her cousin Elizabeth. It is through Mary that Jesus came into that home. In fact, Mary established the reign of Jesus in the house of Zechariah. For at the sound of Mary's voice, Elizabeth was filled with the Holy Spirit. This reign is acknowledged by Elizabeth when she says, under the influence of the Holy Spirit, "And why is this granted me, that the mother of my Lord should come to me?" (Lk. 1:43). The reign of Jesus is a reign of love and mercy poured out by the Holy Spirit and symbolized by His Heart. Thus, Our Lady wishes to bring us closer to the Heart of her Son through the enthronement of His Sacred Heart in the home, and above all, bring us closer to His Eucharistic Heart in the Mass.

5. What else can we learn from the mystery of the Visitation?

Section Two

A mission of mercy

The Visitation of Mary to Elizabeth is both a corporal and spiritual work of mercy to which there must be a response. In the previous mystery of the Annunciation, Mary is the recipient of the Divine Mercy which is infinite. That Mercy came in the form of the Incarnation of Jesus Christ. Through Mary we have all received of that Mercy. Mary speaks of that Mercy in her response to Elizabeth in the *Magnificat*. So it is that Mary herself goes with haste on a mission of mercy. As the Gospel of St. Matthew says: "Blessed are the merciful, for they shall obtain mercy" (5:7).

Corporal work of mercy

What is more evident to us is that Mary goes to Elizabeth on an errand of a corporal work of mercy. This is seen in the fact that Elizabeth was with child in her sixth month and was in need of another's help. Thus, Our Lady sought to help a woman who was with child. It is also true that both Elizabeth and Zechariah were elderly and so weakened by their years. Here Our Lady, while with Child herself, provides us with an example of another work of mercy by coming to the aid of the elderly.

Spiritual work of mercy

Yet there is more. Our Lady visits a family, and not merely to socialize. Mary is on a mission, the mission of the Holy Spirit as a spiritual work of mercy. The Angel had previously told Zechariah that his child would be sanctified in his mother's womb. For the Angel said, "and he will be filled with the Holy Spirit, even from his mother's womb" (Lk.1:15). Indeed, this did occur. On the day that Mary visited the house of Zechariah, Elizabeth remarked that at the sound of Mary's voice the child "leapt for joy in her womb." Elizabeth was "filled with the Holy Spirit" (Lk. 1:41). From the Child Jesus present in the womb of Mary, goes forth the Holy Spirit through Mary to sanctify John. Rather than the ordinary form of the Sacrament of Baptism, the very sound of Mary's voice is an instrument by which the Holy Spirit is imparted to the child John and subsequently to his mother. It is interesting to note that, as in Baptism, John was sanctified in water, but the water of his mother's womb.

Yet with the sanctification of John the Baptist, there was also imparted to him his special mission to prepare the way for the coming of the Lord. When Zechariah later regained his speech, he announced that mission (cf. Lk. 1:76-79). The most important part of Mary's mission to this family is the sanctification of John's soul and the conferring of his mission to prepare the way of the Lord. This was a spiritual work of mercy, and it far surpassed her other numerous corporal works of mercy. It is a work of Mary's spiritual maternity, her maternal love for her children. This family of Zechariah now joins with the Holy Family as a basic building block within the Church. Thanks to Mary's visit, John goes on to build the Church further by providing Jesus with the foundation stones upon which the Church will be built, His first and most important Apostles. We too are called to imitate Mary in bringing the Holy Spirit upon others, for "as each has received a gift," we "...employ it for one another, as good stewards of God's varied grace" (I Pet. 4:10). In particular, we can imitate Mary's role in the sanctification of the family. We can imitate her care for the elderly. We can imitate her care for those mothers who carry a child within them. One way we can address all of these needs is through the apostolate of the Pilgrim Virgin statue and/or the image of Our Lady of Guadalupe.

There is more for us to learn, for we also see in this mystery how we must respond to Mary's maternal love for us. In fact, the Holy Spirit Himself teaches us how we are to respond to our Heavenly Mother by inspiring Elizabeth. Under the influence of the Holy Spirit she says, "Blessed are you among women, and blessed is the fruit of your womb!" (Lk. 1:42, also the *Hail Mary*). The first half of this exclamation, "blessed are you among women," represents words that were addressed only two other times in the Old Testament, to Judith and Jael who both prefigured Mary in her exalted role. Both struck a blow to the head of the enemy of their people. Mary too has struck a blow to the head of the enemy of God's people, that is, "the great dragon" that "was thrown down, that ancient serpent, who is called the Devil and Satan" (Rev 12:9). Also, when we praise Mary and proclaim her victory over Satan with the words of Elizabeth, we are praying in union with the Holy Spirit because these words of praise were inspired by the Holy Spirit. Mary herself responded in the *Magnificat* by saying, "All generations will call me blessed." And so in praying the *Hail Mary* we continue to fulfill that prophecy over and over again in union with the Holy Spirit Who has taught us to say to Mary, "blessed are you among women."

In the second half of the exclamation by Elizabeth, we see how Mary has obtained that victory over evil for us. "Blessed is the fruit of your womb." For Mary has restored to us what was lost by the first Eve in the garden, access to the tree of life. There may be several meanings of the tree of life, but in one sense, Mary is the tree of life which provides us with that blessed fruit Who is Jesus. Mary gives us the Food of eternal life. She gives us Jesus Who remains with us in the Holy Eucharist.

Section Two

Elizabeth continues, "And why is this granted me, that the mother of my Lord should come to me? For behold when the voice of your greeting came to my ears, the child in my womb leaped for joy" (Lk. 1:43-44). Many think they can ignore Mary. Many think they don't need Mary. Yet the Holy Spirit inspires Elizabeth to say that she is not even worthy to receive the visit of Mary into her home. Did those people in Bethlehem know Who they were turning away when they turned away Mary and Joseph? It was Jesus, hidden in Mary's womb. Likewise, today few realize Who they are turning away when they turn away Mary who brings Jesus to us. Yet, we may not turn away some other persons. Poor Mary, who is treated in this way. Won't people open their hearts to her? We beg you; do not permit our dear Mother to be turned away again, lest we turn away her Son Jesus. Rather let us leap for joy that she has come to us with her Son.

Finally, Elizabeth is inspired by the Holy Spirit to say to Mary, "Blessed are you who believed that what was spoken to you by the Lord would be fulfilled" (Lk. 1:45, NAB). Zechariah did not believe. Mary did believe. Yet if Mary did not believe, she would not have consented to the Child Jesus. If she did not consent, she would not have conceived. If Mary did not conceive, we would not be saved. Indeed, Mary, "Blessed are you who believed" (Lk. 1:45, NAB). As St. Augustine taught, by her Faith, Mary conceived Jesus in her Heart before she conceived Him in her body. We are grateful children of Mary. Is there anything else? The following question provides further insight into Mary's visit.

6. Is the mystery of the Visitation prefigured in the Old Testament?

The Ark of the Covenant in the Old Testament

Let us consider the connection of the Ark of the Covenant in the Old Testament with the mystery of the Visitation. The Ark of the Covenant was constructed by the command of God while the people of Israel were still in the desert, having been set free from slavery in Egypt. It was made of wood overlaid with gold. It was like the shape of a box, measuring about 3 feet 9 inches (2.5 cubits) by 2 feet 3 inches (1.5 cubits) by 2 feet 3 inches (this equals a scaled ratio of 25 to 15 to 15), (cf. Ex. 25:10). On the top of the Ark was a plate of gold which was called the "Mercy seat" or propitiatory. Just above the mercy seat was where the presence of God was to be manifested in an extraordinary way (cf. Ex. 25:17-24). The mercy seat was also the place where the sacrifices were to be received by God in reparation for the offenses against Him, and to gain His favor. At the two ends of the mercy seat were placed the images of two cherubim angels each facing one another and the place symbolizing the presence of God, also called the "throne of mercy." Within the Ark was the manna which fed the people in the desert, the two stone tablets of the Ten Commandments, and the rod of Aaron, the brother of Moses and the first high priest of the Mosaic Covenant.

When the Ark was completed and placed in the tabernacle or tent, the cloud of the glory of Yahweh (the *shekinah*) overshadowed the Ark in the sight of the people (cf. Ex. 40:35). The Ark then was visibly at the central place of all worship of God in Israel. On entering the Promised Land, the Ark was carried around the city of Jericho once each day for six days and on the seventh day the Ark was carried around the city seven times and at the seventh time, the seven trumpets sounded, the people shouted, and the walls of Jericho collapsed. The army of Israel attacked and won the victory (cf. Jos. 6:6-21).

The Ark of the Covenant in the Gospel of St. Luke

The Gospel of Luke draws many parallels between the Ark and Mary. The expression that Mary would be overshadowed by the Holy Spirit is the same in the Greek Old Testament for the overshadowing of the Ark of the Covenant (*Septuagint*, Lk. 1:35, Ex. 40:35). Yet the overshadowing of Mary is the fulfillment of what was prefigured by the Ark of the Covenant, the place in which God's presence was honored. The New Ark, Mary, truly contained God substantially present, for "the Word became flesh" in her womb.

By Mary's consent to the Angel Gabriel, a New Covenant was established between God and His people, His bride. Thus the reference to the *Covenant* is to speak of a marriage between God and His people. Mary is the pinnacle of the Church, the Bride of Christ. It is through Mary, this pinnacle, where the union between Christ and His Church is established. This marriage is perpetuated and celebrated in the Wedding Feast of the Lamb, the Holy Mass. Jesus says through the priest, "...for this is the chalice of my Blood, the Blood of the new and eternal covenant..." Thus Mary and the Church are implied as joined to the Bridegroom at this moment. For Mary consented to the Covenant on behalf of the Church at the Annunciation of the Angel.

Not only did Mary consent to the Covenant but as Pope Francis said: "Chosen to be the Mother of the Son of God, Mary, from the outset, was prepared by the love of God to be the *Ark of the Covenant* between God and man" (*Misericordia Vultus*, Bull of Indiction of the Extraordinary Jubilee of Mercy, April, 2015). The Covenant which began with Mary's consent on behalf of mankind was consummated by Jesus on the Cross. "It is finished" (Jn. 19:30). The Bridegroom continues to offer Himself to the Father in the Mass for His Bride without shedding His Blood again. It is one and the same Sacrifice of Himself, the one Victim, but He does not suffer and die again in history. Yet to the Most Holy Trinity, the bloody offering of Calvary is always present.

We see in the Gospel of Luke many more ways in which Mary is to be understood as the new Ark of the Covenant. Luke shows these different ways, especially, in the mystery of the Visitation in which Mary is prefigured by the Ark of the Covenant in the Old Testament. Mary traveled into the hill country of Judea to the house of Zechariah and Elizabeth (Lk. 1:39). The Ark traveled into the hill country of Judea to the house of Obededom (2 Sam. 6:1-11). Obededom was a priest just as Zechariah was a priest. John the Baptist, of a priestly family, jumped for joy in his mother's womb (Lk. 1:43). David was dressed in a priestly ephod as he jumped for joy in the presence of the Ark (2 Sam. 6:14). Elizabeth exclaimed in a loud voice with joy in the presence of Mary and her Son within her (Lk. 1:42). David shouted for joy in the presence of the Ark (2 Sam. 6:15). The word *anephonesin* translated as the exclamation of Elizabeth is used only five other times in the Greek Bible, the *Septuagint*, all in connection with the Ark of the Covenant.

Moreover, Elizabeth said, "And why is this granted me, that the mother of my Lord should come to me?" (Lk. 1:43) David said, "How can the ark of the Lord come to me?" (2 Sam. 6:9). Mary remained in the house of Elizabeth for 3 months (Lk. 1:56). The Ark remained in the house of Obededom for 3 months (2 Sam. 6:11). However, the house of Zechariah was blessed much more than the house of Obededom by the presence of Mary and her Son Incarnate. Also, the word "blessed" is used three times in regard to Mary (Lk. 1:39-45). Obededom's house was blessed by the presence of the Ark (2 Sam. 6:11). Yet the word for "blessed" is used only once. The word for "blessed" is used more in Luke because Mary is the fulfillment of the Ark of the Old Testament and far surpasses it. Mary is more clearly shown to be the New Ark in her Visitation to Elizabeth than elsewhere in the New Testament. Yet, she is in fact the New Ark from the Annunciation to her Assumption into Heaven and for all eternity.

The Ark and the two cherubim

Moreover, on top of the Ark of the Old Testament, the two cherubim faced one another and the "mercy seat," above which the presence of God was honored and manifested through speech and other signs (Ex. 25:10-22, 40:34-38). The "mercy seat" or propitiatory was also the place the

High Priest offered atonement or reparation. First and foremost, this prefigured Jesus, our High Priest, offering Himself in reparation for sin. At the same time, the Ark and the "mercy seat" may be taken as a prefiguration of Mary in whom the High Priest and Victim began to dwell in the flesh. Thus, Jesus, our High Priest and Victim, already began to offer reparation to the Father in the womb of Mary, the New Ark. It is fitting then that we should join ourselves to the Immaculate Heart of Mary in offering reparation to and through the Sacred Heart of Jesus to the Holy Trinity. In this way, Mary is able to be the "mercy seat," the "Mother of Mercy," acting on our behalf through her intercession.

Further, the two cherubim facing one another and the mercy seat of the Ark remind us of the cherubim guarding the tree of life in the garden of Eden (Gen. 3:24). The guarding of the tree of life is a way of saying that the human race had lost access until the coming of the Savior. The tree of life may have several valid meanings. In one sense, Mary is the tree of life and Jesus is the blessed fruit of her womb. Fruit, which is intended to be eaten, is fully realized in the Holy Eucharist. Thus the tree of life lost by Adam and Eve is now restored to us in Jesus and Mary. At the same time, Jesus and Mary are also the New Adam and the New Eve.

The Ark and the Pilgrim Virgin statue

It becomes evident that the Pilgrim Virgin statue, which continues the mystery of the Visitation, is also a representation of Mary who is the Ark of the New Covenant. Since the Ark was a visible sign above which God manifested Himself at the center of public worship, it finds its fulfillment in the Eucharistic Jesus Who was carried in the New Ark. The New Ark, Mary, is joined closely to her Son in the Eucharist at the center of Divine Worship. Thus we have another reason for the fittingness of the Pilgrim Virgin statue going forth from the Mass to the home and then back to the Mass, rather than simply from house to house. Our Lady can also go forth from the Mass to another venue to reach out to the sick and the elderly whose sufferings can be so valuable when offered for the peace and salvation of the world. Our Lady then returns the family to the Mass on the following Saturday. Finally, as we saw above, the Ark is instrumental in a great victory for Israel in the battle of Jericho against a pagan people. So, too, the New Ark will enable us to confront this culture of death. The time has come for the New Ark to bring down the culture of death through the apostolate of her children.

Section Two

7. Is there direct reference to the Ark of the Covenant in the New Testament?

The ark is mentioned for the last time in the last book of the Holy Scripture. "Then God's temple in heaven was opened, and the ark of his covenant was seen within his temple" (Rev. 11:19). This is followed by the words, "And a great sign appeared in heaven, a woman clothed with the sun, with the moon under her feet, and on her head a crown of twelve stars" (Rev. 12:1) Here the Gospel of Luke and the Book of Revelation mutually reaffirm the connection of Mary and the Ark of the Covenant. In the Book of Revelation, reference to the Ark of the Covenant is followed by the great sign, "a woman clothed with the sun." Thus it could be said that the Ark is revealed as the woman who represents Mary. Mary, in turn, is a type and model of the Church.

Mary, the Ark, and the Eucharist

Further, the Ark of the Old Covenant is no longer needed in the practice of our Faith since the Old Covenant ceased to exist with the Incarnation. The Ark of the Old Covenant finds fulfillment in Mary. There remains Mary as the Ark of the New Covenant.

The Ark of the Old Covenant was kept in the Holy of Holies where the high priest carried out what was then the highest form of public worship (cf. I Kings 8:6-8, Hb. 9:3). The Ark of the New Covenant, in turn, directs us to the center of worship, namely, the Holy Eucharist, "the source and summit" of our lives. Thus, the presence of the Pilgrim Virgin statue, the sign of the Ark of the New Covenant and of the mystery of the Visitation (Section Two, q. 6), also signifies the intimate association of Mary and the Eucharist. It is fitting then that the Pilgrim Virgin statue goes forth from the Mass on Saturdays, especially the *First Saturdays*, with those who may have received Jesus in Holy Communion, and so, like Mary, carry Him within themselves.

Further reflection upon Mary as the Ark of the New Covenant will bring to mind many other thoughts about the role of Mary in the Holy Mass. Yet we do so always under the guidance of the teaching of Holy Mother Church, the Catholic Church.

The Book of Revelation and the Book of Joshua

Finally, let us consider again the connection of the New Testament reference to the Ark of the New Covenant in the Book of Revelation and the reference to the Ark of the Covenant concerning the battle of Jericho in the Book of Joshua. After having received the directions given by the Lord, Joshua instructed Israel to march with the Ark around the city walls of Jericho for **seven** days. On the seventh day, the Israelites carried the Ark around the city walls **seven** times. For seven days and on the seventh time around the city walls on the seventh day, the seven priests blew the **seven** trumpets. The people then shouted. The walls of Jericho collapsed. Marching with the Ark of the Covenant, Israel triumphed. Note that there are three distinct sets of seven, the **seven days** of marching around Jericho, **seven times** around Jericho on the seventh day, and the seven priests blew the **seven trumpets** for seven days and on the seventh time around the city on the seventh day (cf. Jos. 6:1-16).

In the Book of Revelation there are **seven seals** of the judgments of God. The seventh seal consists in angels blowing **seven trumpets** of judgments of God (Rev. 8-11). At the blowing of the seventh trumpet, there are voices saying, "The kingdom of the world has become the kingdom of our Lord and of his Christ, and he shall reign forever and ever" (Rev. 11:15). Immediately, the Ark of the Covenant is seen in the temple in Heaven (cf. Rev. 11:19). Finally, during the period of the seventh trumpet, there are the **seven bowls** of God's wrath poured out on humankind (cf. Rev. 16:1-21). It would seem the kingdom of the world is torn down to become the kingdom of our Lord. One might say this is all prefigured by the collapsing of the walls of Jericho as the trumpets are blown seven times.

In both the Books of Joshua and Revelation we see the number seven used in three distinct ways. Yet, the three sevens, in each set of three, are connected in a unique way. In both cases, in the Books of Joshua and Revelation, from the seventh of the first seven follows the second seven, and from the seventh of the second seven follows the third seven. This doesn't seem to be a coincidence.

Also, in the Book of Revelation, one could say that the three sevens corresponding to "the kingdom of our Lord and of his Christ," overcome the three sixes, which represent "the kingdom of the world." In the midst of this battle stands the Virgin Mother of God symbolized by the Ark of the Covenant. Our Lady, the New Ark of the Covenant, seen in the temple in Heaven, seems to have triumphed.

8. Does the Ark of the Covenant prefigure anything else?

Above, we considered the text from the Book of Revelation: "Then God's temple in heaven was opened, and the ark of his covenant was seen within his temple" (Rev 11:19). In this verse, the Ark is Mary. This has been established in the Gospel of Luke and contained within Sacred Tradition. The Ark of the Old Testament represents Mary and even continues to do so in Heaven for eternity. This representation is not in the manner of an icon which bears a resemblance to a person, but rather in the form of a symbolic representation. Further, in expressing "the ark of the covenant" in words, we refer to Mary by a metaphor. This is similar to the way we would refer to Jesus by a metaphor, e.g., "Lion of Judah."

The Ark and the Holy Eucharist

In addition to what has already been said about the Ark of the Covenant, Scripture tells us, "Behind the second curtain stood a tent called the Holy of Holies, having ... the ark of the covenant covered on all sides with gold, which contained a golden urn holding the manna, and Aaron's rod that budded, and the tables of the covenant" (Heb. 9:3-4). All of this may have an additional meaning. What might these contents mean and what might these contents suggest about Mary herself? First, the Ark contains the manna with which God fed His people in the desert. In the Gospel of John, Jesus Himself talks about the manna which fed the people in the desert (Jn. 6:49). He tells us that this manna prefigured Himself as the "Bread of Life." It follows then that just as the Ark of the Old Covenant carried the manna, the Ark of the New Covenant, Mary, carries Jesus, the "Bread of Life" and the blessed Fruit of her womb. This title of Ark of the Covenant, as found in the Litany of the Blessed Virgin Mary (cf. *The Communal First Saturdays Devotional*, Part I, 2.25), also indicates that Mary is inseparable from her Son in the Holy Eucharist and that she enables us to receive Him in the Eucharist more fruitfully.

The Ark and the Word made Flesh

There were other articles found in the Ark which prefigure the Incarnation. There were two stone tablets upon which were written the Ten Commandments. According to Pope Benedict XVI, speaking on the Solemnity of the Assumption in 2011, the two stone tablets in the Ark "manifested the will of God to maintain the covenant with his people, indicating to them the conditions to be faithful to God's pact, to conform themselves to the will of God and thus also to our most profound truth." But Mary as the ark, he said, received Jesus in herself: "the whole content of the will of God, of the truth of God; she received in herself him who is the new and eternal covenant." In other words, the tablets also represent Jesus as the Word made flesh within Mary.

The Ark and the priesthood

Finally, the rod of Aaron was kept in the Ark of the Covenant. Remember that Aaron was a priest and his rod blossomed miraculously. (cf. Num. 17:8). The rod of Aaron represents the priesthood of Jesus which He assumed at His miraculous Conception. The priest is a mediator, and Jesus became a mediator through the assumption of human nature at His Conception with Mary's consent. God does not mediate outside of Himself by reason of His Divine Nature but by reason of the human nature assumed by the Son of God.

The Ark and the Heart of Mary

Yet, does this tell us anything more about Our Lady as the Ark of the New Covenant? In carrying Jesus in her womb, Our Lady had the real presence of God in the flesh within her. In this way, Our Lady surpasses the old Ark of the Covenant which signified the presence of God. Yet, there is more to being the Ark of the New Covenant. To carry Jesus spiritually is greater than to carry Him physically. Remember the woman who cried out, "'Blessed is the womb that bore you, and the breasts that you sucked!" But he said, 'Blessed rather are those who hear the word of God and keep it!'" (Lk. 11:27-28). Our Lady heard the word and consented to it. St. Luke also tells us that Mary kept all these things in her heart (cf. Luke 2:19, 51). She kept Jesus and everything about Him in her Heart as no other human being ever did. In Jesus is the fullness of grace and truth, and she received Christ in her Heart more than any other mere creature. Mary stands apart from all other mere creatures because she is the Virgin Mother of God and was never the enemy of God, but immaculate from the first moment of her conception. Thus, Mary is the image and unique tabernacle of Christ. "…it is no longer I who live, but Christ who lives in me" (Gal. 2:20). In fact, one could say about the latter words that, in a sense, it was never Mary who lived but Christ who lived within her because she was conceived in the state of grace. St. Augustine also affirms that Mary conceived Jesus in her Heart by Faith before she conceived Him in her body (Serm. CCXV, 4 in PL 38, 1074). It is the Holy Spirit, given to Elizabeth at the sound of Mary's voice, Who inspires Elizabeth to exclaim, "…blessed is she who believed…" (Lk 1:45). Thus, we could say that the Immaculate Heart of Mary is also the Ark of the Covenant.

The Ark and reparation by the Immaculate Heart of Mary

Section Two

What then are we to say of that form of spiritual union with Jesus that perfects Faith? Faith leads to the greater virtue of Hope. Yet perfection can only be achieved by Love in the heart. Yet Love inspires reparation. Just as the "mercy seat" of the Ark was a place of atonement or reparation, so the Immaculate Heart of Mary is like the "mercy seat" or "propitiatory" on which reparation was and is offered to God. The victim offered upon the mercy seat is Jesus Himself. This began when the Father sent His only begotten Son into the womb of Mary, the New Ark. Yet, she first conceived Jesus in her Heart as St. Augustine said. One could say that Jesus was already offering Himself to the Father upon the mercy seat of Mary's womb. One could also say that Our Lady was already offering Jesus to the Father in her Immaculate Heart. As Our Lady carried Jesus close to her Heart, she came into the temple to offer the Victim to God, the Victim Who Simeon announced would be "a sign that will be contradicted" (Lk. 2:34, *NAB*).

Yet, Our Lady acted as the advocate of the entire human race by offering the Victim to the Father and continues to do so. For Jesus is a light to the Gentiles, who together with the Jews, represent the entire human race (cf. Lk. 2:32). In continuing as our advocate, Our Lady receives our offering to God. When we totally consecrate ourselves to Our Lady, we entrust to her the meritorious and reparatory value of all our good works (cf. *The Communal First Saturdays* book, Part II, Section One, Ch.1, q. 5). Mary in turn presents these to Jesus on our behalf. Again, Our Lady is like the "mercy seat" on which we offer reparation to the Father through Jesus in the unity of the Holy Spirit.

At the same time, Mary is a person to whom we try to make reparation for the sins that offend her. As it has been said, this is a matter of justice in regard to our own sins and a matter of mercy when trying to make reparation for the sins of others that offend the Immaculate Heart of Mary. We must keep in mind that any reparation for sins against the Immaculate Heart of Mary is reparation primarily made to God Who is offended by all sin. We offer reparation to the Holy Trinity upon the Ark of the New Covenant even for those sins which offend the Ark of the New Covenant itself, Mary. Recall the priest who was punished for unlawfully touching the Ark of the Covenant. One could say that reparation to the Immaculate Heart of Mary through the *First Saturdays* helps to fulfill the meaning of the Ark of the Covenant. It is important to note that we try to make reparation to the Immaculate Heart of Mary so that a more complete reparation can be made to the Sacred Heart of Jesus Who out of His Love gave us His Mother. It is important to say again that all reparation must ultimately be to the three Persons in one God.

The Ark of the New Covenant is the Heart of Mary

The Heart of Mary is both the dwelling place of God as well as the propitiatory where sacrifice is offered. For these reasons, it is especially true to say that the Ark of the New Covenant is the Immaculate Heart of Mary. "Then God's temple in heaven was opened, and the ark of his covenant was seen within his temple..." (Rev. 11:19). In reflecting on this text for the Solemnity of the Assumption, Pope Benedict XVI said, "Thus the New Testament tells us that the true ark of the covenant is a living and concrete person: it is the Virgin Mary. God does not dwell in a piece of furniture, God dwells in a person, in a heart..." In the Book of Revelation then, it could be said that what appears in Heaven, is the Immaculate Heart of Mary as the Ark of the New Covenant, the one true and worthy place where Jesus resides. In the Heart of Mary, Jesus finds a permanent and perpetual residence spiritually. As the Ark of the Covenant from its very beginning was reverenced as a place of God's presence, so the Immaculate Heart of Mary, the New Ark of the Covenant, from her very beginning, was the dwelling place of the Holy Trinity. Unlike the rest of mere humanity, there was never any enmity between God and Mary. Nor can there be found among any of God's mere creatures a spiritual relationship such as the one that exists between Mary and her Son. Yet, where the Son dwells, there also we find the Father and the Holy Spirit. Thus, the Father and the Holy Spirit also dwell together with the Son in Mary's Heart as in no other mere creature.

The Ark seen in Heaven

Yet, why do we see the Immaculate Heart of Mary in Heaven as represented by the Ark of the Covenant in the Book of Revelation? We have seen already in question 7 that this scene is prefigured in the Book of Joshua. There we saw that the Ark of the Covenant was taken around Jericho for **seven days**. The Ark was taken around the city once each day until the seventh day. On the seventh day, the Ark was brought around the city walls **seven times.** On the seventh time around Jericho, **seven trumpets** were blown, and after the people shouted, the walls collapsed (cf. Jos. 6:1-20). In the Book of Revelation, the Lamb opened **seven seals** portending a series of significant events (cf. Rev. 6-8). With the opening of the seventh seal, the Angels blew **seven trumpets** in succession (cf. Rev. 8-11). It is at the blowing of the seventh trumpet and "loud voices" that the Immaculate Heart of Mary appeared in Heaven represented by the Ark of the Covenant, and then "a great sign appeared in heaven" (cf. Rev. 11:15-12:1). The great sign of the woman is commonly understood to be Our Lady (on the 50th anniversary of the apparitions at Fatima, Blessed Paul VI wrote an Apostolic Exhortation called *Signum Magnum, The Great Sign*). Here we see the close association of the Ark of the Covenant with the Great Sign which is Our Lady. The Great Sign appears at the beginning of the period of the seventh trumpet. Later, during the period of the seventh trumpet, the **seven bowls** of God's wrath are poured out on humanity (cf. Rev. 16:1-21).

Just as there were seven days, on the seventh day seven times around Jericho, and on the seventh time seven trumpets were blown, so there are seven seals, from the opening of the seventh seal the blowing of seven trumpets, and from the seventh trumpet seven bowls following the appearance in Heaven of the New Ark of the Covenant, Mary. Just as with the Ark of the Covenant Israel triumphed, so **the Immaculate Heart of Mary will triumph** as she promised at Fatima and as it is possible to interpret from the book of Revelation (cf. Rev. 11:19-12:1). The triumph of the Immaculate Heart of Mary is a triumph of Our Lord. "The kingdom of the world" is replaced by "the Kingdom of our Lord and of his Christ" (Rev. 11:15). While there can be many valid meanings to these passages, the triumph of the Immaculate Heart of Mary is one possibility.

The Ark and the home

It is thanks to Mary that, by the mediation of her Immaculate Heart, the Holy Trinity is able to reside in us by grace, and we hope the Holy Trinity will do so as never before among the people of all nations. We thus await the triumph of the Ark as the Immaculate Heart of Mary. One way that helps us on the journey to this triumph is by bringing into the home, the "Ark of the New Covenant" as represented by the Pilgrim Virgin statue. Truly, especially in the mysteries of the Annunciation and the Visitation, we see Mary as the fulfillment of the Ark of the Covenant. In the Pilgrim Virgin statue as a representation of the Ark of the New Covenant, we find a continuation of these mysteries in our lives, which can ultimately lead us through Mary's Heart to the Heart of Jesus and, in the next life, Heaven itself. Fittingly, the high point of Our Lady's visitation in the home or other venue is the enthronement of the Sacred Heart of Jesus. Yet, most important, with our return to the church on Saturday, Our Lady leads us to the Eucharistic Heart of Jesus in the Mass. It is in the Holy Mass that the meaning of the Ark of the Covenant is fully realized. The Litany of Loreto, said after the First Saturday Mass, can serve as a reminder of the Ark of the Covenant and its meaning.

9. Does the Pilgrim Virgin statue represent anything else?

After being joined in prayer with our Blessed Mother, the Apostles went forth as the "Pilgrim Church" (*Redemptoris Mater*, n. 25-26) from the upper room, moved by the Holy Spirit to preach the Good News (cf. Acts 2:1-24). For this reason, we may see in the Pilgrim Virgin statue a representation of the Pilgrim Church which brings the Gospel and the graces of the Holy Spirit to the whole world. Further, the above Encyclical Letter presents the Virgin Mary at the head of the Church's pilgrimage of Faith (cf. *Redemptoris Mater,* n. 25). This theme carries throughout the entire Encyclical. Thus the Pilgrim Virgin statue reminds us of Mary's and the Church's pilgrimage of Faith.

It is interesting to note that the inspiration for the Pilgrim Virgin goes far back in history to the 9th century. One of the pilgrim routes to the shrine of St. James the Apostle, Santiago de Compostela, came from Portugal and passed through Pontevedra, Spain where Our Lady and her Son requested the *First Saturdays*. Pious tradition tells us that in those early days of the pilgrimage, Our Lady appeared among the pilgrims on the way from Portugal to Santiago de Compostela. To commemorate this, the Pilgrim Virgin chapel was built at Pontevedra in the 19th century. It seems fitting then that the *Communal First Saturdays* should include a Pilgrim Virgin statue to be sent out from the church following the Mass (cf. Section Two, q. 14). In addition, the flagship of Christopher Columbus, the Santa Maria, which carried a statue of Our Lady, was built in Pontevedra, and so one could say began its journey to America from there.

10. Why would the Pilgrim Virgin statue go forth from and return to the First Saturday Masses and the other Saturday Masses?

It is perfectly fine for the Pilgrim Virgin statue simply to travel directly from one house to another. In doing this Our Lady is able to fulfill her mission of bringing the Fatima message and blessing the home abundantly. Nonetheless, it is most fitting that the Pilgrim Virgin statue should go forth from every Mass on Saturday or at least from the *First Saturdays* Mass. As we shall see, the visit of the Pilgrim Virgin statue from church to home provides additional ways of understanding Mary's visit.

Before Our Lady visited Elizabeth, Jesus became incarnate within her. In the Mass, Jesus becomes present in the Holy Eucharist and is received in Holy Communion. At the end of the Mass, the faithful, who may have received Jesus, are sent out into the world. The Pilgrim Virgin statue fittingly goes forth from the Mass symbolizing the People of God going forth as the "salt of the earth" and the "light of the world." The statue is able to represent this because Mary herself is the model of the Church and she represented the Church at the Annunciation in giving her consent.

It is also true that the Pilgrim Virgin statue can call to mind the Ark of the Covenant, which was the place where God manifested Himself at the center of the liturgical worship of the people of Israel. Yet, when sacrifice was not being offered upon the mercy seat, the Ark was often traveling from one place to another through the desert or land of Israel before the temple was built. It is fitting then that the Pilgrim Virgin statue should move from the celebration of the Eucharistic Liturgy and return to the Eucharistic Liturgy.

Further, the Pilgrim Virgin statue is able to go forth again from the Mass to signify Mary's desire to bless the home. Our Lady blesses the home especially by helping to establish the reign of the Sacred Heart of Jesus in the home by the enthronement. After the Pilgrim Virgin statue remains in the home for a week, the host returns the statue to the parish on the following Saturday before the morning Mass. By leading the members of the household back to the Mass, Our Lady accomplishes the most important part of her mission.

Finally, the Pilgrim Virgin statue has a special affinity with the 15 minute meditation on the Word after the First Saturday Mass. The *lectio divina* meditation in the *Communal First Saturdays* ends with the beginning of the mystery of the Visitation as its "action" step (cf. also Pope Benedict XVI, *Verbum Domini*). "In those days Mary arose and went with haste into the hill country, to a city of Judah" (Lk. 1:39). Mary acted upon the inspired Word of the Angel by going with haste to the home of Elizabeth who was elderly and with child. Likewise, on the *First Saturdays*, the "action" step of the meditation provides a meaningful transition to the reception of the Pilgrim Virgin statue which begins with a reenactment of the mystery of the Visitation in the church (cf. *The Communal First Saturdays Devotional* book, Part I, 2.24, 3).). On other Saturdays, the Pilgrim Virgin statue is received immediately following Mass with a brief reflection. On those other Saturdays, the reenactment of the mystery of the Visitation takes place in the home.

11. Who brings the Pilgrim Virgin statue to the home or other venue?

A coordinator of the Pilgrim Virgin statue schedules those who wish to have the statue in their homes. Also, a custodian of the Pilgrim Virgin statue is in charge of the recommended reception after Mass, as well as welcoming the statue that is returned to the church before Mass. In addition, the custodian may replenish a possible accompanying case with approved religious articles and various media helpful to the family in learning the message of Fatima (cf. "Recommendations for the Week-long Visit" on pages 11-13 of this book).

Further, it is the one hosting the Pilgrim Virgin statue who will ordinarily receive the statue after the Mass on Saturday. The host receives the statue in the above-mentioned reception of the Pilgrim Virgin statue in the church, and then brings the statue home or to another approved venue. Families and apostolates are encouraged to participate in the reception and return of the Pilgrim Virgin statue.

12. Is it permitted to have more than one Pilgrim Virgin statue?

A parish may have as many Pilgrim Virgin statues as are required to meet the needs of the parishioners. Thus it is possible that after beginning with one statue, a need may arise for additional statues. This also may include the image of Our Lady of Guadalupe for the Pro-Life apostolate. Much of what has been said about the Pilgrim Virgin statue may be applied to the image of Our Lady of Guadalupe. For example, since Our Lady of Guadalupe is with Child, Mary shows us how she is a fitting fulfillment of the Ark of the Covenant. Also, by Our Lady of Guadalupe's appearance to Juan Diego, while with Child, does she not bring to mind the mystery of the Visitation?

When these additional statue(s) and/or image(s) are brought to the church, it is recommended that they be covered before, during, and after Mass. In this way, the focus of attention may be given to one statue. This would be helpful to one's prayer.

13. May a household receive the Pilgrim Virgin statue if there is already a statue of the Virgin Mary in the dwelling?

A household may receive a Pilgrim Virgin statue into the household even if there is already a statue present. It would be fitting though that the Pilgrim Virgin statue be located in the place of honor, and the other statue be placed in another room. It is recommended that the Pilgrim Virgin statue be placed at the location where the Sacred Heart of Jesus would be enthroned.

14. Is the Pilgrim Virgin statue necessary to the Communal First Saturdays?

Section Two

The Pilgrim Virgin statue visitation is not necessary for the fulfillment of Our Lady's request for the *First Saturdays,* whether done individually or communally. Nonetheless, the *Pilgrim Virgin Statue Church to Home Visitation* devotion does support the *First Saturdays* and its mission of peace and the salvation of souls. The visitation does this by supporting the entire Fatima message of which the *First Saturdays* is an essential and most urgent part. *The Pilgrim Virgin Statue Church to Home Visitation* devotion gives this support by encouraging the practices of the Fatima message. The Visitation also does this by leading the faithful to the enthronement of the Sacred Heart of Jesus in the home or other venue.

The Pilgrim Virgin Statue Church to Home Visitation establishes a connection between the local church and the domestic church, between the Mass and the world. *The Pilgrim Virgin Statue Church to Home Visitation* devotion is more directly connected with the *Communal First Saturdays* by helping the faithful recognize that the *First Saturdays* Mass is a source from which the Pilgrim Virgin goes forth as well as the summit and destination to which she returns with the family. Thus, the *Pilgrim Virgin Statue Church to Home Visitation* devotion is meant to encourage and invite the faithful to participate in the *Communal First Saturdays*.

This same Pilgrim Virgin statue can go forth from and return to the other Saturday Masses, providing the occasion of encouraging and inviting participation in the *Communal First Saturdays*. This participation, in turn, can promote the fulfillment of one's obligation to participate in the Sunday and holy day Masses. For these reasons, the *Communal First Saturdays* includes the *Pilgrim Virgin Statue Church to Home Visitation* as an important part of the entire *Communal First Saturdays* devotion.

15. Does the visit of the Pilgrim Virgin statue of Our Lady provide a form of outreach from the Communal First Saturdays?

When the Mass is ended, people are sent out to bring Christ into the world. An option we have for the *Communal First Saturdays* is to also send out a Pilgrim Virgin statue of Our Lady as a symbol of this, and in fact, to bring the Gospel Message into the world primarily through the basic social unit of society and the Church, the family. More specifically, a Pilgrim Virgin statue of Our Lady represents the mystery of Mary's visit to Elizabeth. In this visit to Elizabeth's home and family, Mary carried the Child Jesus within her, bringing the Gospel and an abundance of blessings to that home. The visit of the Pilgrim Virgin statue may be an occasion of many blessings, including the message of the Gospel, for the home and family. "If the Church has accepted the message of Fatima, it is above all because that message contains a truth and a call whose basic content is the truth and the call of the Gospel itself" (Pope John Paul II, homily at Fatima, May 13, 1982).

During the visit of the Pilgrim Virgin statue for a week, the household is encouraged to pray the Rosary every day. It is also recommended that the image of the Sacred Heart of Jesus be enthroned in the home as a sign that He reigns in that home, and as a sign that the family is the domestic church (cf. *Catechism of the Catholic Church*, n. 1655-1658). This special place of prayer for the family provides an outward sign of the domestic church. It would also be ideal to place an image of the Immaculate Heart of Mary and an image of St. Joseph beside the image of the Sacred Heart of Jesus. In these ways, after her visit, Our Lady helps leave behind a more permanent blessing in the home. Shall the Lord "not open the windows of heaven for you and pour down for you an overflowing blessing"? (Mal. 3:10).

16. Are there other ways that the Pilgrim Virgin statue visitation may be an apostolate of the Communal First Saturdays?

A Pilgrim Virgin statue can also be sent to nursing homes and the sick. Elizabeth was quite old when Mary visited her. The Pilgrim Virgin statue visitation provides a possible beneficial occasion to bring Holy Communion to the elderly and sick, and help them practice the *First Saturdays* in a communal form. This devotion helps the elderly and the sick to realize that there is a very great deal that they can do for the Church in their weakness. Because of the weakened condition of the elderly and the sick, the order of devotion for the *Communal First Saturdays,* at the nursing home, can be appropriately shortened to fulfill simply the four practices of the *First Saturdays* (cf. Appendix B of *The Communal First Saturdays* book). Confession, one of these practices, can be provided for even more than eight days from the First Saturday (Jesus to Lucia, February 15, 1926). The Rosary could be prayed before the reception of Holy Communion and the additional meditation on the mysteries of the Rosary could be fulfilled after Holy Communion.

Further, not only should the elderly and the sick offer these practices in reparation to the Sacred Heart of Jesus and the Immaculate Heart of Mary, but they also should be encouraged to offer their suffering in reparation to the Hearts of Jesus and Mary. This reparation by the elderly and the sick consoles the Hearts of Jesus and Mary and, at the same time, helps obtain the graces of salvation for a multitude of souls. This emphasis on the value of suffering as a practice of the *Communal First Saturdays* outreach helps provide the elderly and infirm with a mission of extraordinary value. The infirmity then which could depress them becomes an occasion of great joy.

Moreover, since Mary assisted Elizabeth who was carrying her child, a Pilgrim Virgin statue or an image of Our Lady of Guadalupe may be brought to a place where Our Lady may save the life of the unborn and/or inspire repentance in those who are about to sin or have sinned against life. The Pilgrim Virgin statue or an image of Our Lady of Guadalupe may also visit places where women with child are being counseled and provided for. Also the Pilgrim Virgin statue or an image of Our Lady of Guadalupe may visit places where women who have had abortions are receiving assistance in the healing process. It is even possible to bring the Pilgrim Virgin statue or an image of Our Lady of Guadalupe to keep vigil at an abortion clinic. It is said that many women turn away from their appointments for abortions when there are people praying outside. Thus the Pilgrim Virgin statue or an image of Our Lady of Guadalupe can be of great assistance in Pro-Life activities. The presence of the Pilgrim Virgin statue or an image of Our Lady of Guadalupe can be a sign of Our Lady's continuing care for those like Elizabeth who was with child. Further, the Pilgrim Virgin statue or an image of Our Lady of Guadalupe is a reminder of the love Our Lady offers sinners by her message of hope and salvation.

Further, the Pilgrim Virgin order of devotion can also be used at the Pro-Life place of destination. Again, one may substitute the Pilgrim Virgin statue with an image of Our Lady of Guadalupe. The Pilgrim Virgin statue or image of Our Lady of Guadalupe would need to be returned to the designated guardian on the same day unless the statue or image stays for a week in a permanent place of Pro-Life apostolate or a home. In the latter case, it would then be possible to practice the same order of devotion during a week-long visit as practiced in the home, including the enthronement of the Sacred Heart of Jesus.

In these ways and others, the visitation of the Pilgrim Virgin statue of Our Lady or an image of Our Lady of Guadalupe provides an outreach from the *Communal First Saturdays* and possibly each Saturday celebration of the Mass in order to help transform the world into a "civilization of love" and a "culture of life." Our Lady's image ever invites us to take up our Rosary to meditate on the life, death, and glory of her Son in her company. Our Lady's week-long journey is complete when the household or apostolate brings the statue or image back to the Mass on Saturday. Yet, should we not say that Our Lady returns the household or apostolate back to the celebration of the Mass?

17. Why say the Rosary in the home, the church, or elsewhere?

The members of the home or other entity are asked to say the Rosary every day before the Pilgrim Virgin statue. We have good reason to love Our Lady since she is the Mother of God and our Mother. We know that Our Lady deserves to be honored and that graces come through her. Yet, it is even more important to love our Blessed Mother. When we love someone, do we not seek to give them what is pleasing to them as well as what is truly good? Persons who truly love others put aside what is merely pleasing to themselves but seek to learn what is pleasing to the beloved. When we consider those apparitions approved by the Church, it is clear that Our Blessed Mother is greatly pleased by the devotion of the Holy Rosary.

Yet it is also true that the Church itself has frequently recommended the Holy Rosary to us and adorned it with many indulgences as further incentive for its recitation. There have been more encyclicals written on the Rosary than any other devotion. We especially recommend that the faithful read *Rosarium Virginis Mariae* by St. John Paul II. We also join with St. John Paul II in recommending *The Secret of the Rosary* by St. Louis de Montfort. We can always be sure that in responding to the recommendations of Mother Church that we are responding to Our Lady herself who is both Mother and model of the Church. One could also say that the Motherhood of the Church is an extension of Our Lady's Motherhood in our midst. Thus, the Church extends to us Our Lady's Maternal care for us in asking us to take up her Rosary. Yet, why is the Rosary recommended so strongly?

The development of the Rosary

Historically, the Rosary has its roots in the 150 Psalms of David. The first half of what is now the Hail Mary was substituted for each Psalm as a devotion of the faithful said using Paternoster beads. So it became known as the Psalter of Our Lady. The Order of Preachers, under the patronage of St. Dominic, played a major role in the development of the prayer. By the end of the 15th century, there were 15 decades and mysteries for meditation. At this time, the prayer came to be called the Rosary since each Hail Mary was like a rose offered to Mary to form a crown of roses. In more recent times the Popes have referred to the Rosary as the Gospel prayer because the Rosary is a summary of what God has revealed, a summary of our Faith. This latter title calls to mind how helpful the Rosary is in calling to mind the principal mysteries of our Faith. St. John Paul II recommended the addition of five Luminous mysteries to the fifteen mysteries to make the Rosary even more comprehensive of the Gospel (*Rosarium Virginis Mariae*). St. John Paul II also recommended that we make use of Scripture in meditating on each mystery (*ibid*). Our use of Scripture in saying the Rosary and the use of the *lectio divina* for the *Communal First Saturdays* should be very helpful in this regard. The Rosary then has become an increasingly more powerful instrument of prayer.

The Rosary has a body and a soul

It may be said that the Rosary has a body and a soul. The vocal prayers represent the body of the prayer. The meditation on the mysteries represents the soul of the prayer. In this way, the Rosary resonates with human nature itself which is composed of a body and a soul. In this way, the Rosary engages the entire being of the person which needs to be entirely offered to God. Together with the vocal prayers, even the fingers are employed with the beads. These are the more external parts of the prayer and tend to engage the body of the person. The soul of the Rosary consists in the meditation upon the possible 20 mysteries. These engage the interior part of the person, the heart and even the soul itself. Thus the Rosary engages the entire person.

Because the entire person is engaged in the Rosary, the person who prays is more fully challenged than in many other forms of prayer. This accounts for the greater difficulty that many will experience in praying the Rosary. Yet a person of any age or level of spiritual development may take up the Rosary and progress from there.

The Rosary and spiritual fitness

One may understand the Rosary better by a comparison to physical fitness. One of the goals of physical fitness is to develop a stronger and therefore healthier body. The word for strength in Latin is *virtus* from which we derive the word virtue. One of the objects of saying the Rosary is to develop all the virtues which might be thought of as the muscles of the soul. In exercising these virtues with the help of grace, we can make our way to Heaven.

Now the quickest method of building strong muscles is through various exercises. These exercises require repetition. When the person uses weights in the performance of these exercises, the muscles are challenged to overcome the resistance of the weights. Over time, the muscles are being forced to grow and become stronger.

The Pilgrim Virgin Statue Church to Home Visitation

The Rosary might be called a form of spiritual exercise to develop spiritual muscles, namely the virtues. It too requires repetition, especially evident in the body of the prayer. Like physical fitness, the Rosary can be very challenging because a kind of total effort is required. In fact, those who desire to grow great physical strength use the heaviest weights that a given amount of repetition allows. Because the Rosary so thoroughly engages the whole person, it may be said that it is a method of prayer that engages the heaviest weights. This means that the Rosary is capable of producing great virtue, and is able to do so in a shorter period of time. Moreover, it is an exercise we can take up almost anywhere at anytime, even in the darkest dungeon.

The Rosary and the Hearts of Jesus and Mary

Our Lady came to Fatima as Our Lady of the Rosary, revealing her Immaculate Heart. With or without any words, Our Lady joined the Rosary devotion and devotion to her Immaculate Heart together. Even if she had not done so, it would be possible to see the great benefit of doing so. Devotion to the Rosary can be devotion to the Immaculate Heart of Mary. The reason is that "Mary kept all these things, pondering them in her heart" (Lk 2:19). Whenever Scripture refers to Mary pondering in her Heart, she is pondering a mystery also found in the Rosary. We may surmise from this that Mary pondered all the mysteries that are found in the Rosary. These mysteries of the Rosary and even the words found in the prayers are dear to Mary's Heart. Yet, the Heart of Mary is not only the receiver of God's word and His mysteries, but her Heart also represents for us the love she has for God and for us. Mary's love is the key to the Heart of Jesus in every mystery. The love represented by her Heart explains everything she does in these mysteries and can join us to the Heart of Jesus, her Son. Further, Our Lady is pleased when she sees Jesus' Heart at the center of each mystery within our hearts. Also, Jesus is pleased when He sees that our hearts become like Mary's Heart as well as His own. So, it is possible to join the devotion to the Sacred Heart of Jesus and the Immaculate Heart of Mary with the devotion of the Rosary.

Further, there are various ways devotion to the Rosary can be joined with devotion to the Immaculate Heart of Mary. First, by the Rosary we can begin to live our consecration to the Sacred Heart of Jesus through the Immaculate Heart of Mary. Second, Our Lady asked us to say the Rosary in reparation to her Immaculate Heart, which is primarily reparation to the Sacred Heart of Jesus. Third, by meditation on the mysteries of the Rosary, we can ponder the ways in which we may imitate the Immaculate Heart of

Section Two

Mary and learn how we may better relate to the Sacred Heart of Jesus. Having pondered the Immaculate Heart of Mary in whom we see Jesus in these mysteries, we can ask for the grace to love Jesus as she did. Finally, by bringing the devotion of the Rosary and the devotion to the Hearts of Jesus and Mary together, the power of the devotion of the Rosary and the power of the devotions of the Hearts of Jesus and Mary are combined to produce an even greater power to obtain the graces of the Holy Spirit.

18. Why is the body of the Rosary necessary if the soul of the prayer, the meditation, is more important?

It has already been said that the vocal prayers form the body of the Rosary and the meditation on the mysteries is the soul of the prayer. The body and soul of the Rosary more fully engages the body and soul of the person than do many other forms of prayer. Thus, the whole person becomes a prayer to God.

Repetition and love

Yet there are other considerations as well. It has been said, why all this repetition of vocal prayers? We have seen how both fitness and virtue (a good habit) are developed through repetition. Another way of conceiving of this is that as Bishop Sheen said, a person never tires of hearing the words, "I love you." So we say "I love you" over and over to Our Lady in saying the Hail Mary. We do the same in repetitious prayers to Jesus. Also, Our Lord Himself showed us the importance of repetition as He repeated His prayer to the Father three times in the garden. We know also that He said or sang the Psalms which are plentiful with repetitious phrases.

Repetition and impressions on the mind

In today's advertising there is a great deal of repetition because they understand the psychological effectiveness of doing this. We may even find ourselves in need of an antidote for this repetitious advertising. That antidote is especially found in the Holy Rosary. If we trace a circle in the ground with a stick, each time we repeat that same circle we make a deeper impression. So each of the words of the Hail Mary and other prayers are more deeply impressed upon our memory. Think of each of those words such as Mary, grace, Jesus, etc. These words are now more likely to float to the surface of our consciousness.

Repetition calms the mind

Something else results from the repetition of the vocal prayers of the Rosary. Anything that is repetitive can have a calming effect on the mind. The repetition of the Rosary has just such a calming effect on the mind. Yet the fact that we express these prayers outwardly in varying degrees keeps us alert at the same time. Even so the calming effect of the Rosary permeates the mind and the entire being. Thus it is like seeing large waves on a lake gradually diminish until the water becomes very still. We are then able to look down into the depths. So with the repetition of the vocal prayers in the Rosary, the mind is rendered more disposed to a deeper consideration of the mysteries of God. Again this form of prayer is rather unique as well as challenging.

Repetition provides a holy environment

Further, we can all understand the value of having a clean, healthy, and beautiful environment. What if we were able to create our own spiritual environment? One example of doing this might be when we play beautiful religious music in the background while we are in a conversation with a friend. While we give our primary attention to our conversation with our friend, the sacred music, nonetheless, creates a mood or feeling that may be helpful to the conversation. It could be said that we do this when we say the vocal prayers of the Rosary as the metaphorical music in the background for our meditation on the mysteries. This meditation includes our conversation with the Lord and His Mother. A prayer that creates its own spiritual environment is something unique to this devotion and a great advantage. Also it could be said that Mary herself is the perfect environment in which to ponder Jesus in our hearts. Such is the Hail Mary. In all of the above explanations of the vocal prayers, it is true as St. Thomas Aquinas says, "grace builds on nature."

Vocal prayers keep time

Moreover, the vocal prayers act as a kind of timing device for our meditation. The vocal prayers counted on our beads provide us with a consistent period of time devoted to meditation each day. We can devote ourselves to the meditation without needing to look at a clock to see what time it is. Often when a person simply meditates on some mystery, it can be very difficult to have a sense of the passage of time.

Section Two

Our Father

Finally, each of the vocal prayers is quite important in itself. For example, the Our Father is the prayer Jesus taught us. It is a perfect prayer. Its seven petitions contain all that we need and in the order that we need them. The Our Father should be more for us than simply a vocal prayer. Rather, we should very carefully meditate on the Our Father itself apart from the Rosary. It is not enough to impress the words upon our memory. Rather, through meditation, we need to impress the wonderful order of the Our Father upon our intellect and will.

Hail Mary

Yet, why are there so many Hail Marys? It must be remembered that when God wished to renew the world, He sent the Angel Gabriel to Mary. It is St. Gabriel's greeting that becomes the basis for the Hail Mary. It is through this greeting that God wishes to continue to renew the face of the earth. This prayer helps us focus on the blessed fruit of her womb, Jesus. In the end, it is the powerful intercession of Our Lady with her Son that is obtained through the Hail Mary and the Holy Rosary.

19. Why should we meditate on the mysteries of the Rosary?

Some may say that meditation is too difficult. Yet, many spend a great deal of time meditating or thinking about other things that are not of a religious nature. They even think about how they are going to do the things they think about and desire. There is no good reason then that we can't give the same attention to the things of God. In fact, St. Alphonsus Ligouri said that we must practice mental prayer if we wish to be saved. It is through meditation that we are able to dwell on the reasons for living a virtuous life. Through persevering in this meditation we are able to grow in the virtues. The mysteries of the Rosary provide us with one of the richest sources and example of virtuous living upon which to meditate. Such virtuous living is necessary for our salvation.

However, it is not possible to meditate on something we don't understand. Thus it follows that we need to learn about the scriptural sources for the mysteries. In addition, explanations of most of the mysteries of the Rosary may be found in Part One of the *Catechism of the Catholic Church* explaining the Nicene Creed. The Rosary also calls to mind most of the Sacraments in the mysteries. We can read about the Sacraments in Part Two of the *Catechism*. Moreover, the Rosary contains moral and virtuous acts in all the mysteries. We can read about this in Part Three of the *Catechism*. Finally, the Rosary is itself a prayer. We can read about prayer in Part Four.

Also, the *Communal First Saturdays* provides a way of meditating on the mysteries by employing *lectio divina* with Scripture. Our Lady asked for an additional meditation on the mysteries of the Rosary for 15 minutes on the *First Saturdays*. It could be said that one reason for this was that Our Lady wanted to strengthen our ability to meditate when we say the Rosary. Also, it could be said that knowing the scriptural background of the mysteries of the Rosary is essential to improving our ability to meditate on the mysteries. The *Communal First Saturdays* is able to provide this help to the faithful in the form of *lectio divina*.

Reflecting on the mysteries of the Rosary helps to prepare us for a deeper participation in the Liturgy, and especially the Mass. In the Mass, these very mysteries are presented anew and perpetuated. Also after Mass, meditation on these mysteries, as practiced in the *Communal First Saturdays,* helps us to benefit more fruitfully from the real presence of the Eucharistic Jesus within us. Since the Real Presence of Jesus remains within us for a period of time, we should try to consciously remain with Him for at least a little while whenever we receive Him. Otherwise, there is a danger that we may walk away forgetful of Who we carry within us. Meditating on the mysteries of the Rosary after Mass will help to bring to life our awareness of Jesus' Real Presence within us. This awareness will also help promote our reverence toward Jesus in the Holy Eucharist in subsequent Masses. Moreover, our reflection upon the mysteries of the Rosary helps us to relate more deeply to the various seasons of the liturgical calendar to which the various parts of the Rosary correspond.

Finally, it should be no surprise that at Fatima Our Lady said, "Pray the Rosary every day." In telling us to pray the Rosary, Our Lady is also asking us to meditate on the mysteries of the Rosary. So, as one important answer to the original question as to why we should meditate on the mysteries of the Rosary, we can simply say that Our Lady asked us to do so.

20. Why say the family Rosary?

"Again I say to you, if two of you agree on earth about anything they ask, it will be done for them by my Father in heaven. For where two or three are gathered in my name, there am I in the midst of them" (Mt 18:19-20). Jesus' words imply that our prayer can have a greater power when we pray to God with others. Also Jesus is present when one is joined in prayer with others. This doesn't mean that Jesus is not present to the individual when he is alone. Rather in coming together in His name, there is an added form of spiritual presence and power. This fuller presence finds its roots in the truth that God is Himself three Divine Persons in one God, a Community of Persons. It is also true that we are not only made in the image of the one God, but also in the image of God Who is Three Persons in one God.

Image of the Holy Trinity

Yet this image of the Holy Trinity is not only found in the individual but also in the family. This is our fundamental community of persons in society and the Church. As a result, other social groups are able to bear the image of God as well. Yet, when the gathering is centered on Jesus Christ, the group can be perfected by the grace of the Holy Spirit. The social group can then be both the image and likeness of the Holy Trinity. Individuals then, made in the image of the Holy Trinity, find a fulfillment of the meaning of their very being in coming together with others in the Name of Jesus Christ. In the family or in any communal gathering in which we say the Rosary, we are in fact coming together in prayer and in the Name of Jesus Christ.

Domestic church

Not only is Jesus present, but the whole Christ is present in some way in the family. The reason is that the family, in coming together in the Name of Christ, shows that it is truly the domestic church. As the domestic church, the family represents the entire Church or Body of Christ, the whole Christ.

Further, it may be said that other communal gatherings are also ways which bear visible witness to the presence of the Body of Christ, the Church. These communal gatherings reach greater perfection in the gathering of the local church and especially in union with the bishop(s) of the diocese in liturgical celebrations. The greatest prayer and sacrifice of all is the Holy Mass. The Holy Eucharist is the "source and summit" of our lives. This is because the Body and Blood of the new and eternal covenant is in the Holy Eucharist. As a covenant between God and His people, the Eucharist is the wedding feast of the Bridegroom and His Bride. It is in the wedding feast of the Holy Mass that the community is able to reach its highest state in this life as the image and likeness of the Holy Trinity. The family is also called to join in that greater community of the Church, especially in the Holy Mass. It is important to recognize that the family Rosary is an excellent way to dispose family members to the ultimate prayer and sacrifice found in the Holy Mass.

Praying together outside the Liturgy

Yet, even though we attend Mass every week, and possibly by an additional grace every day, our Faith should permeate all of our time throughout the day. One would not likely even attend the obligatory Mass each week if he or she had no other form of spiritual nourishment during the week. What can be done to cultivate the spiritual life of the people when they are not attending the Liturgy? We need ways to strengthen us during the entire day and week. Devotional gatherings as well as private devotions can help in this regard. The Rosary, in particular, is a prayer in which all can join with one another as, for example, in the family or pray alone, whether young or old, educated or uneducated. It is a prayer in which we contemplate Mary carrying Jesus, the Son of God, within her. It is a prayer through which Mary always leads us to Jesus, even to the foot of the Cross. It is a prayer in which Mary prepares us to be more fruitfully united with her Son in the Holy Eucharist and so follow Him into eternal life. Thus, the people of God need to be encouraged to find ways, such as the Rosary, to extend their communion with God throughout the day and every day.

The family Rosary is particularly important in this regard since the family is the fundamental social unit of the Church and society. It is there in the family that life begins. It is there in the family that we are first formed and educated. Aristotle had said that a small error in the beginning is a great error in the end. The family is the beginning of civilization and so must be strengthened against error in that beginning. The Rosary is a tremendous help to the family in staying on the right path. The Rosary helps to foster family unity in Faith and Love. "The family that prays together stays together."

The Rosary evangelizes the family

Yet the unity of the family has been attacked and broken down in our times. It is time for a *new evangelization* that begins with the family as well as the individual. The Rosary itself is referred to by the Order of Preachers as a method of preaching because it continues to evangelize us day after day as we open ourselves to the truth of the mysteries of our Faith. Thus, let every family learn to pray the Rosary together and so be transfigured by the grace of God through the prayers of our Blessed Mother.

The family Rosary best meets the needs of all members

Section Two

Finally, one might still say that it is better to say the Divine Office, also referred to as the Liturgy of the Hours. The Liturgy of the Hours together with the seven Sacraments comprise the Liturgy or the official public worship of the Church. The preeminence of the Liturgy is all quite true without any doubt. However, we must distinguish between what is objectively better in itself and what is subjectively better for a given person or group. Generally speaking, a family is composed of members of varying age, ability, and stage of development. For example, a child seven or less years of age would not ordinarily be expected to participate within a family saying the Divine Office because it requires reading and a much larger vocabulary. However, the child could actively participate in the family Rosary. At a much earlier age a child is able to learn and pronounce the Our Father and the Hail Mary and can therefore participate. In addition, the little one can learn the mysteries in a simple way. Thus, the Rosary is able to impress the sacred words and mysteries upon the innocent heart of the child in a way that is compatible with his receptivity.

On the other hand, the prayers and mysteries of the Rosary can never be fully comprehended by the greatest theologians because the prayers and mysteries infinitely surpass the human capacity to comprehend them fully. For those who do say the Divine Office, the Rosary should have a place in their spiritual life. Not only does the Rosary help to fulfill one's obligation of devotion to the Mother of God, but it also serves as a kind of mirror of the Liturgy at those times outside liturgical celebration. Also, canon law asks that the Rosary be fostered among the students in formation for the clerical state (n. 246, 3). Finally, we have wonderful models of saying the Rosary in our recent Popes. For example, St. John Paul II called the Rosary his "favorite prayer." In fact, both St. John Paul II and St. John XXIII were known to say at least fifteen decades of the Rosary every day.

21. What are the fifteen promises of the Rosary?

The following are the 15 promises of Mary to Christians who recite the Rosary *(attributed to St. Dominic and Blessed Alan de La Roche).*

1. Whoever shall faithfully serve me by the recitation of the Rosary, shall receive signal graces.

1. I promise my special protection and the greatest graces to all those who shall recite the Rosary.

2. The Rosary will be a powerful armor against hell. It will destroy vice, decrease sin and defeat heresies.

3. It will cause virtue and good works to flourish; it will obtain for souls the abundant mercy of God; it will withdraw the hearts of men from the love of the world and its vanities, and will lift them to the desire of eternal things. Oh, that souls would sanctify themselves by this means.

4. Those who recommend themselves to me by the recitation of the Rosary shall not perish.

5. Whoever shall recite the Rosary devoutly, applying himself to the consideration of its sacred mysteries shall never be conquered by misfortune. God will not chastise him in His justice, he shall not perish by an unprovided death; if he be just, he shall remain in the grace of God, and become worthy of eternal life.

6. Whoever shall have a true devotion for the Rosary shall not die without the Sacraments of the Church.

7. Those who are faithful to recite the Rosary shall have during their life and at their death, the light of God and the plentitude of His graces; at the moment of death they shall participate in the merits of the saints in paradise.

8. I shall deliver from Purgatory those who have been devoted to the Rosary.

9. The faithful children of the Rosary shall merit a high degree of glory in Heaven.

10. You shall obtain all you ask of me by the recitation of the Rosary.

11. All those who propagate the holy Rosary shall be aided by me in their necessities.

12. I have obtained from my Divine Son that all the advocates of the Rosary shall have for intercessors the entire celestial court during their life and at the hour of death.

Section Two

13. All who recite the Rosary are my sons, and brothers of my only Son, Jesus Christ.

14. Devotion to my Rosary is a great sign of predestination.

22. Is it possible to gain a plenary indulgence by praying the Rosary or in fulfilling the First Saturdays?

The following is an excellent explanation of what one must do to gain indulgences. It is taken from The *Gift of an Indulgence* by the Apostolic Penitentiary and based on the *Enchiridion Indulgentiarum*, Fourth Edition, July 1999 (for more information cf. *Manual of Indulgences*, 2006, USCCB).

1. This is how an indulgence is defined in the Code of Canon Law (can. 992) and in the *Catechism of the Catholic Church* (n. 1471): "An indulgence is a remission before God of the temporal punishment due to sins whose guilt has already been forgiven, which the faithful Christian who is duly disposed gains under certain prescribed conditions through the action of the Church which, as the minister of redemption, dispenses and applies with authority the treasury of the satisfactions of Christ and the saints".
2. In general, the gaining of indulgences requires certain prescribed conditions (below, nn. 3, 4), and the performance of certain prescribed works.
3. To gain indulgences, whether plenary or partial, it is necessary that the faithful be in the state of grace at least at the time the indulgenced work is completed.
4. A plenary indulgence can be gained only once a day. In order to obtain it, the faithful must, in addition to being in the state of grace:
— have the interior disposition of complete detachment from sin, even venial sin;
— have sacramentally confessed their sins;
— receive the Holy Eucharist (it is certainly better to receive Jesus while participating in Holy Mass, but for the indulgence only Holy Communion is required);
— pray for the intentions of the Supreme Pontiff.
5. It is appropriate, but not necessary, that the sacramental Confession and especially Holy Communion and the prayer

for the Pope's intentions take place on the same day that the indulgenced work is performed; but it is sufficient that these sacred rites and prayers be carried out within several days (about 20) before or after the indulgenced act. Prayer for the Pope's intentions is left to the choice of the faithful, but an "Our Father" and a "Hail Mary" are suggested. One sacramental Confession suffices for several plenary indulgences, but a separate Holy Communion and a separate prayer for the Holy Father's intentions are required for each plenary indulgence.

6. For the sake of those legitimately impeded, confessors can commute both the work prescribed and the conditions required (except, obviously, detachment from even venial sin).

7. Indulgences can always be applied either to oneself or to the souls of the deceased, but they cannot be applied to other persons living on earth. [*The Gift of the Indulgence,* Apostolic Penitentiary, 29 January, 2000, www.vatican.va].

The complete detachment from sin necessary to gain a plenary indulgence and mentioned in n. 4 is expressed in different words by the act of contrition provided in Part I, 2.14 of *The Communal First Saturdays Devotional* book, which says, "I detest all my sins…" This should be taken to mean all venial as well as mortal sin. This detachment from sin is not a feeling but simply an act of the will.

The Communal First Saturdays and indulgences

We can see that the *Communal First Saturdays* offers a wonderful opportunity to gain a plenary indulgence either for oneself or for the souls in Purgatory. As we have seen, the *Communal First Saturdays* include the Rosary. To gain a plenary indulgence, one may say the Rosary "in a church or oratory" alone or with others as one of the prescribed works. One could also say the Rosary anywhere "with members of the family, in a religious Community, or in a pious association" (cf. *Manual of Indulgences, 2006*). The Rosary is said within a group of people and in a church as part of the *Communal First Saturdays*. This Rosary certainly qualifies as one of the prescribed works for a plenary indulgence while the other conditions are included in the *Communal First Saturdays*, such as Confession, reception of Holy Communion, and prayers for the Holy Father. As mentioned above,

Section Two

one of the acts of contrition found in *this* book may be used to remind one to detest consciously all sin, mortal and venial (cf. 2.14).

Other ways of gaining plenary indulgences

Other works that may gain a plenary indulgence every day are a half hour of reading or listening to the Scripture, a half hour of adoration of Jesus in the Holy Eucharist whether in the tabernacle or exposed, or making the Stations of the Cross in an approved manner. Each of these works must include all the other conditions mentioned in n. 4 in the quotation above. One may fulfill the half hour of Scripture outside of a church and alone.

It could be said that the *Communal First Saturdays* includes the essence of all of these other ways of gaining a plenary indulgence, at least in part. Some may even fulfill the 15 minute meditation for the *First Saturdays* with the Stations of the Cross as a meditation on the Sorrowful Mysteries of the Rosary, especially because one meditates on the Carrying of the Cross and the Crucifixion of Jesus. However, if one only did the Stations of the Cross for the meditation on the *First Saturdays* each month, one would never meditate on the other mysteries of the Rosary. This does not seem to be what Our Lady had in mind. Rather, the *lectio divina* offers us the opportunity to meditate on the possible 20 mysteries of the Rosary, at least over a period of several or more *First Saturdays*. When we do this privately, we have the option of extending the meditation to 30 minutes so that we can gain the plenary indulgence for Bible reading. This would be helpful when we can only say the Rosary alone and outside of a church or chapel.

As we can conclude from above, saying the Rosary alone and outside of a church or chapel would not qualify for a plenary indulgence, whereas the 30 minute Scripture reading/meditation can be done alone and outside of a church or chapel to qualify for a plenary indulgence. Also, during the *Communal First Saturdays*, the 15 minutes spent in meditation after Mass is ordinarily spent in the presence of the Holy Eucharist. This would only require another 15 minutes to qualify as one of the works specified to gain a plenary indulgence. However, this would not be necessary to gain a plenary indulgence if the Rosary was already said in the church. There are also other ways of gaining a plenary indulgence on special days and occasions, such as Divine Mercy Sunday (cf. *Manual of Indulgences*, 2006). One may gain only one plenary indulgence per day except on the day of one's death, one may then gain two plenary indulgences (cf. *Manual of Indulgences, 12.2,4)*.

In addition to the other conditions, one would need to go to Confession within about 20 days before or after the prescribed work in order to be assured of the possibility of gaining a plenary indulgence every day (cf. n. 5). So, by going to Confession once a month for the *First Saturdays*, one is able to gain a plenary indulgence every day, provided one fulfills the other conditions daily.

Church esteem for the practices of the First Saturdays

As can be seen, the Church is already giving special encouragement to the kinds of practices contained in the *Communal First Saturdays* by granting plenary indulgences for them as a way of motivating people to practice these particular devotions as well as the conditions. This shows us that the Church holds such works in high esteem. By including some of these devotions and practices in a single devotion, the *First Saturdays* offers a devotion of even greater efficacy. At the same time, one is able to fulfill the requirements for the plenary indulgence. Yet one may be able to fulfill the *First Saturdays* without gaining the plenary indulgence or vice versa. It is important to note that one may gain a partial indulgence for any good work throughout the day by any prayer or good work done with that intention.

Charity toward neighbor

In any case, the gaining of plenary indulgences or even partial ones can be an excellent way to practice charity and mercy toward one's neighbors, namely, those in Purgatory. One need only make the intention to apply the indulgence to oneself or those in Purgatory. One can be sure that the person released from Purgatory will intercede on one's behalf from Heaven. It is important to note that one who is totally consecrated to Jesus through Our Lady according to the de Montfort way, has already given the indulgence to her so that she may apply it in the best possible way. St. John Paul II supports this devotion of total consecration: "I would like to recall among the many witnesses and teachers of this [Marian] spirituality, the figure of St. Louis Marie Grignion de Montfort, who proposes consecration to Christ through the hands of Mary, as an effective means for Christians to live faithfully their baptismal commitments" (*Mother of the Redeemer*, n. 48, brackets are ours).

Section Three

Questions on the Enthronement of the Sacred Heart of Jesus and the Placement of the Images of the Immaculate Heart of Mary and St. Joseph

23. What is the enthronement of the Sacred Heart of Jesus?

To enthrone literally means to place someone upon a throne. The common practice is to give the word enthronement a more special meaning. By the enthronement of the Sacred Heart of Jesus, we wish to acknowledge that we have but one King and Head of the Mystical Body. Jesus is Divine and only the Father and the Holy Spirit are equal to Him. All creation is subject to Him. In addition, enthronement involves installing an image of the Sacred Heart of Jesus, if possible, in a place where the faithful can pray together on a daily basis in a house or other place. The enthronement represents that the Sacred Heart of Jesus truly reigns by love over our homes and in our hearts as King and Friend. We not only can recognize Jesus' supreme authority over us, but also can symbolize by His image that He is what is most important in our life and that He is first in our lives. Jesus is "Alpha and the Omega, the first and the last, the beginning and the end" (Rev. 22:13). In seeking Jesus first, we seek His kingdom. "But seek first his kingdom and his righteousness, and all these things shall be yours as well" (Mt. 6:33). In this way, we put our life and house in order.

In particular, we enthrone the image of the Sacred Heart of Jesus to be a reminder that He is full of love and mercy toward us at all times. Through faith in this love of Jesus for us, the entire family can be enfolded and joined as one in this love. Further, the image of the Sacred Heart of Jesus in the home is a visible and permanent sign that the household is a domestic church. As a domestic church, the home is a place where God is worshiped and where the household joins in common prayer. In addition, the domestic church is a place where the members love and respect one another. In turn, the members of the domestic church can become aware of their obligation to reach out and so bring the love they have experienced to others.

24. Why does the visit of the Pilgrim Virgin statue in the home culminate in the enthronement of the Sacred Heart of Jesus?

Our Lady who wishes to establish the reign of her Son and His Kingdom wherever she goes. Our Blessed Mother always wishes to lead us to Jesus. Mary wants us to know Jesus' infinite love for us and His unfathomable Mercy. He is always the source and goal of her mediation on our behalf. The New Eve is always saying to Jesus, "...They have no wine" (Jn. 2:3). She always tells us, "...Do whatever he tells you" (Jn. 2:5). Jesus in turn, will always tell us, "Behold, your mother!" (Jn. 19:27) It is only fitting then that Our Lady lead us to the Sacred Heart of Jesus by the enthronement of His image in the home. Another way of saying this is that Our Lady brings Jesus into the home to establish the reign of the Sacred Heart of Jesus in the home. It is also fitting then that we place an image of our Mother and Queen beside that of the Sacred Heart of Jesus. Our Blessed Mother can remind us of how we should respond to the Sacred Heart of Jesus with love. By looking into her Heart, we can learn how we should love Him. Our Lady's image also reminds us of her Maternal love for us. Finally, we are reminded of our need to depend on her mediation with her Son.

Although the enthronement of the Sacred Heart of Jesus is the high point of Our Lady's visit to the home, her mission does not end there. Our Lady's mission is primarily to bring us to her Son and His Real Presence in His Body, Blood, Soul, and Divinity in the Holy Eucharist. For the greatest Gift of love of the Sacred Heart of Jesus to us is the Holy Eucharist.

On Saturday, Our Lady returns to the church with the family, so she can bring the family into the presence of her Son in the Holy Mass. The visit of the Pilgrim Virgin statue, from beginning to end, can be contemplated in the mystery of the Visitation. The visit of the Pilgrim Virgin statue may hopefully call to mind Our Lady's visit to the home of Zechariah and Elizabeth. When Our Lady brought Jesus into that home and at the sound of her voice, "...Elizabeth was filled with the Holy Spirit" (Lk. 1:41). Elizabeth not only acknowledged the reign of Jesus by calling Him Lord but she also acknowledged His Real Presence in the womb of Mary (Lk. 1:42-43). So we acknowledge the reign of Jesus by the enthronement of His Sacred Heart and by reverencing His Real Presence in the Holy Eucharist when we return to the church.

Since the Pilgrim Virgin statue is scheduled to be received after the Mass on Saturday and to return just before the Mass on the following Saturday, it is recommended that the family be present for the Mass as well. When the Saturday falls on a First Saturday, the family will also have the opportunity to fulfill Our Lady's request for the *First Saturdays*.

25. How do we prepare for the enthronement of the Sacred Heart of Jesus?

In preparation for the enthronement of the Sacred Heart of Jesus, the following steps are recommended:

Section Three

First, prepare a place for the Pilgrim Virgin statue, and nearby, a place for the Image of the Sacred Heart of Jesus to be enthroned later in the week, as well as places for the other images of the Immaculate Heart of Mary and St. Joseph. These places could be the mantel over the fireplace, a suitable space on a wall, or a table for this purpose. These prepared places could be in a location where the family or faithful could pray on a daily basis.

Second, set a date for the enthronement of the Sacred Heart of Jesus. The Friday following the reception of the Pilgrim Virgin statue is most fitting, since Friday is the day dedicated to the Sacred Heart of Jesus and the day of Our Lord's death on the Cross and our redemption. Also, another reason Friday is a good day for the enthronement is that we have most of the week to prepare. A third reason is that the enthronement is the crowning event in the home.

Third, obtain pictures of the Sacred Heart of Jesus, the Immaculate Heart of Mary and St. Joseph. The image of St. Joseph should always remind us how we should love Jesus and Mary. Ensure that the images have been blessed beforehand if a priest or deacon will not be present at the enthronement. If one wishes to hang the pictures on the wall, it would be good to have the necessary picture hooks in place beforehand. For the actual enthronement, one might want to have another small table where one may lay the images before carrying them to the home altar or other prepared place.

Fourth, before receiving the Pilgrim Virgin statue on Saturday, it is recommended that the members of the home or other venue attend the Mass that morning, and if on the First Saturday, attend the *Communal First Saturdays.*

Fifth, follow the order of devotion for the *Pilgrim Virgin Statue Church to Home Visitation*, "On Entering the Home" and "Recommendations for the Week-long Visit" (cf. Section One, 2.) and 3.)

Sixth, meditate on the meaning of the enthronement and how important it is to you and your loved ones (cf. Section Three, q. 23-28).

Seventh, consider inviting relatives and friends to be present for the enthronement. By inviting others, you can begin to be an apostle of the Sacred Heart of Jesus and the Immaculate Heart of Mary.

It is suggested, if possible, that all members of the household or apostolate attend Mass on the day of enthronement, receive Holy Communion with the intention of making reparation to the Sacred Heart of Jesus, and petition Him for the graces of the enthronement. The family or apostolate might try to attend the next First Friday Mass in reparation to the

Sacred Heart of Jesus as well as try to attend the next *Communal First Saturdays* (cf. Section Three, q. 26).

The host might ask the parish priest or deacon to preside at the enthronement, but this is not required, and may not be possible. Ordinarily, the head of the household or some other member would preside if a priest or deacon is not present.

26. What are some of the promises of the Sacred Heart of Jesus to St. Margaret Mary?

Jesus loves us immensely and has laid down His life for us. Devotion to the Sacred Heart of Jesus is a response to this love. Our love in response to Jesus is the act of the greatest virtue we can practice in this life, charity. Further, Jesus promised to St. Margaret Mary certain graces to those who practice devotion to His Sacred Heart. It is to be noted that those who enthrone the Sacred Heart of Jesus in their homes (cf. q. 23) may be the beneficiaries of almost all of the following promises. Also, the enthronement, as it is practiced in the *Pilgrim Virgin Statue Church to Home Visitation*, includes the principal acts of devotion to the Sacred Heart of Jesus, consecration and reparation (cf. *Miserentissimus Redemptor,* Pius XI).

Some promises of the Sacred Heart of Jesus

The following writings concerning some promises of the Sacred Heart of Jesus in response to those who devote themselves to His Sacred Heart were taken from *The Letters of St. Margaret Mary Alacoque* (translation authorized by the Monastery of the Visitation, Paray-le-Monial, France, TAN) and other writings:

> The zeal you show in making the Sacred Heart of our divine Master known and loved will draw down upon you more and more the fullness of His pure love (To Mother Dubysson, Letter 116, p. 177).

> A lesser soul would not be strong enough to turn aside the just wrath of God, so great are the crimes committed. I hope the Divine Heart will be an inexhaustible source of mercy for it. That, I think, is what He promised the good Father de la Colombiere (To Mother de Saumaise, Letter 97, p. 140).

Section Three

He made me understand that the ardent desire He had of being loved by men and of drawing them from the path of perdition into which Satan was hurrying them in great numbers, had caused Him to fix upon this plan of manifesting His Heart to men, together with all Its treasures of love, mercy, grace and sanctification and salvation. This He did in order that those who were willing to do all in their power to render and procure for Him honor, love, and glory might be enriched abundantly, even profusely, with these divine treasures of the Heart of God, which is their source. It must be honored under the symbol of this Heart of flesh, Whose Image He wished to be publicly exposed. He wanted me to carry it on my person, over my heart, that He might imprint His love there, fill my heart with all the gifts with which His own is filled, and destroy all inordinate affection (To Fr. Croiset, Letter 133, p. 230).

He then seemed to promise her "that all those who are devoted to this Sacred Heart will never perish and that, since He is the source of all blessings, He will shower them in abundance on every place where an image of this loving Heart shall be exposed to be loved and honored (To Mother de Saumaise, Letter 35, p. 47).

He has strengthened me in the conviction that He takes great pleasure in being loved, known, and honored by His creatures. This pleasure is so great that, if I am not mistaken, He promised me that all those who are devoted and consecrated to Him will never be lost. Since He is the source of all blessings, He will shower them in abundance on every place where a picture of His divine Heart shall be set up and honored. He will reunite broken families, will protect and help those who are in any necessity and those who approach Him with confidence. He will pour out the sweet unction of His ardent charity on every religious community that honors Him and places itself under His special protection. He will turn aside the blows of divine justice so as to restore to grace those who have fallen from it (To Mother Greyfié, Letter 36, p. 50).

Strive especially to get religious communities to embrace it [devotion to the Sacred Heart Jesus], for they will draw so much help from it that they will need no other means to bring them back to their first fervor. It will restore the most exact observance in the most lax communities and bring to the height of perfection those who live a truly observant life.

The laity will find in this lovable devotion all the helps necessary for their state in life: peace in their families, consolation in their work, the blessing of heaven on all their undertakings, consolation in their afflictions. It is especially in this Sacred Heart that they will find a refuge during their whole life and principally at the hour of death. O, how sweet it is to die after having practiced a tender and constant devotion to the Sacred Heart of Jesus Christ!

My divine Master has made known to me that those who labor for the salvation of souls will work with the greatest success and know how to touch the most hardened hearts if they have a tender devotion to His Sacred Heart, and strive to instill it in others and to establish it everywhere.

Finally, it is perfectly clear that there is no one in the world who would not receive every kind of help from heaven if he had a truly grateful love for Jesus Christ. It is such a love one shows by practicing devotion to His Sacred Heart (To Her Director [Father Rolin or perhaps Father Croiset, Letter 141, pp. 267-8, brackets are ours).

More and more He is disclosing to His unworthy slave His great longing to be known, loved, and honored by men in reparation for the great bitterness and many humiliations they have made Him suffer. He wishes to apply to them the merits of His sufferings in this way.

He shows how great is this longing of His by promising that all those who consecrate themselves to Him and are devoted to Him in order to give Him this pleasure, who do all in their power to give Him and cause others to give Him all the love, honor, and glory they can by the means He provides, will never be lost. He will be their secure refuge against all the snares of their enemies. Especially at the hour of death this divine Heart will receive

Section Three

them lovingly and make their salvation sure (To Fr. Croiset, Letter 131, p. 202).

There is nothing sweeter or more gentle and at the same time stronger or more efficacious than the unction of the ardent charity of this lovable Heart. To convert the most hardened sinners and penetrate the coldest hearts He will make the word of His preachers and of His faithful friends like a flaming sword. It will melt by His love the coldest hearts (To Fr. Croiset, Letter 132, p. 222).

One day He appeared to me covered with wounds and told me to look at the opening of His sacred side which was a bottomless abyss made by a spear beyond all measure, the spear of love… It was in this abyss that I had to disappear. It was the dwelling place of all his friends, wherein they would find two lives: one for the soul and one for the heart. The soul finds in it the spring of living water to purify itself and receive the life of grace of which sin had deprived it. The heart finds in it a burning furnace of love which lets it live only through love… But as its entrance is small one has to be small and devoid of everything to enter into it (Writings to Mother de Saumaise, no. 22, p. 143, as cited in *The Promises of Our Lord to St. Margaret Mary: A textual, theological and pastoral study*, Wenisch).

Embrace the cross lovingly, whenever it comes, as the most precious token of love I can give you in this life (Writings to Mother de Saumaise, no. 44, p. 154, as cited in *The Promises of Our Lord to St. Margaret Mary: A textual, theological and pastoral study*, Wenisch).

I promise you, in the excessive mercy of My Heart, that Its all-powerful love will grant all those who communicate on nine consecutive first Fridays of the month the grace of final repentance. They will not die in My disfavor nor without receiving their sacraments. My divine Heart shall be their secure refuge in their last moments (To Mother de Saumaise, Letter 86, p. 120, bold is ours).

Also, in practicing the *First Fridays* devotion, the faithful may offer their Holy Communion in *Reparation* for the sins which have offended the Eucharistic Heart of Jesus. This will help to fulfill our obligation to make reparation to the Sacred Heart of Jesus as far as possible. (Cf. *Devotion to the Sacred Heart*, Fr. Croiset S.J., TAN, 1988, p. 183. Fr. Croiset was the spiritual director of St. Margaret Mary. Also cf. *Miserentissimus Redemptor*, Pius XI, n. 12, May 28, 1928.)

> He has, moreover, promised His unworthy slave that, if she gives herself over completely to loving Him, He Himself will pray to His Father for those who recommend themselves to her prayers.
> How can I ever enumerate, my dear Mother, all the mercies of this loving Heart? Notwithstanding my ingratitude, He has never shown me greater or more wonderful ones. I consider myself nothing but an obstacle to the furthering of His glory and the imparting of His Grace to souls because of the tepid life I lead. This often makes me the object of His just wrath (To Mother de Saumaise, Letter 86, p. 120).

The role of reparation in obtaining the promises of the Sacred Heart of Jesus

Pope Pius XI referred to consecration to the Sacred Heart of Jesus as a duty in which we return love to Jesus Who loves us (cf. *Miserentissimus Redemptor*). Yet, acts of reparation are also a duty and have a more special place in the devotion to the Sacred Heart of Jesus according to Pope Pius XI:

> And truly the spirit of expiation or reparation has always had the first and foremost place in the worship given to the Most Sacred Heart of Jesus, and nothing is more in keeping with the origin, the character, the power, and the distinctive practices of this form of devotion, as appears from the record of history and custom, as well as from the sacred liturgy and the acts of the Sovereign Pontiffs (*Miserentissimus Redemptor*).

It is to be noted that "reparation has always had the first and foremost place in the worship given to the Most Sacred Heart of Jesus." It would also be true that reparation has the first and foremost place in devotion to the Immaculate Heart of Mary. Through consecration and reparation to the Immaculate Heart of Mary, we can more perfectly worship the Sacred Heart of Jesus. Thus, to more perfectly worship the Sacred Heart of Jesus, we would want to fulfill what Jesus and His Mother have requested. We are reminded that St. John Paul II and the bishops fulfilled the first of Our Lady's two special requests, the consecration of Russia to the Immaculate Heart of Mary. It would seem reasonable that the Church would give at least equal attention at the proper time to the second special request by recommending and promoting the *First Saturdays* in reparation to the Immaculate Heart of Mary. This second special request was emphasized even more by Jesus and Mary than the first special request for the consecration of Russia.

Possible devotions in reparation to the Sacred Heart of Jesus that would obtain many of the above promises are:

- Making and renewing an act of consecration to the Sacred Heart of Jesus.
- Receiving Holy Communion frequently in the state of grace.
- *First Fridays*: receiving the Eucharist on the First Friday of each month for nine consecutive months as stated in the above promises, in bold letters. Some parishes and communities offer public First Friday devotions.
- Private *First Fridays*. If public *First Fridays* are not available, one can still fulfill them privately by receiving Holy Communion on that day. In addition, there is the opportunity to offer one's Communion in reparation for the offenses against the Eucharistic Heart of Jesus. In case of serious sin since one's last Confession, one must go to Confession before receiving Holy Communion.
- If one is unable to attend a First Friday Mass, one may substitute another day as early as possible, receiving Holy Communion with the intention of making reparation to the Sacred Heart of Jesus (cf. Fr. John Croiset S.J., spiritual director of St. Margaret Mary, *The Devotion to the Sacred Heart,* ch. III). It is suggested that one might do this on the First Saturday by offering one's Communion in reparation to the Sacred Heart of Jesus and the Immaculate Heart of Mary.
- A Holy Hour: Eucharistic Adoration for one hour on Thursdays or some other day ("...could you not watch with me one hour?" Mt. 26:40). A Holy Hour can be made alone or as part of a group with

formal prayers (cf. Pope Pius XI, *Miserentissimus Redemptor*, n. 12).
- Enthronement of the Sacred Heart of Jesus in the home.
- Celebrating the Solemnity of the Sacred Heart of Jesus (see below).
- Devotion to the Divine Mercy. This devotion may be considered a further development of devotion to the Sacred Heart of Jesus. This devotion contains many particular practices, including the Chaplet of Divine Mercy (cf. *The Diary of St. Faustina Kowalska*).
- Fulfilling the *First Saturdays* devotion. Reparation to the Immaculate Heart of Mary is part of reparation to the Sacred Heart of Jesus. The two Hearts must reign together side by side. Also, it is important to note that the Sacred Heart of Jesus pours out His graces to us through the mediation of the Immaculate Heart of Mary (cf. *The Communal First Saturdays* book, Part II, Section One, Ch. 1, q. 5). Thus, the devotion to the Sacred Heart of Jesus includes the intercession of the Immaculate Heart of Mary.
- Corporal and spiritual works of mercy in reparation to the Sacred Heart of Jesus. These acts together with all other acts of virtue may be summed up in the third principal act of devotion to the Sacred Heart, imitation. Thus, we speak of three principal acts of devotion to the Sacred Heart of Jesus, consecration, reparation, and imitation.

Note also that the feast of the Divine Mercy is on the first Sunday after Easter. Also, June is devoted to the Sacred Heart of Jesus, and the Solemnity of the Sacred Heart of Jesus is ordinarily celebrated during that month on the Friday after the Solemnity of the Most Holy Body and Blood of Christ, together with the liturgical celebration of the Immaculate Heart of Mary on the next day.

27. May the enthronement be accompanied by the placement of an image of the Immaculate Heart of Mary in the home?

From a previous question on the enthronement, it should be clear that we are using the words enthronement and throne differently. As already mentioned, by the enthronement of the Sacred Heart of Jesus we wish to acknowledge that we have but one King of love and Head of the Mystical Body. Jesus is Divine and only the Father and the Holy Spirit are equal to Him. All creation is subject to Him. Jesus is "the first and the last" (Rev. 22:13). In Jesus is the fullness of authority. Since Jesus has these unique prerogatives, we would reserve the word enthronement for the Sacred Heart of Jesus.

Section Three

As a metaphor, we would understand the word throne to signify a person's royal dignity. Through Baptism, we participate in the royal dignity of Jesus as King. You are "a royal priesthood" (I Pet. 2:9). The Apostles are said to sit upon 12 thrones "judging the twelve tribes of Israel" (Lk. 22:30). Yet, there are even more important thrones in Heaven as we can see from the following passage. These thrones are those of Mary and Joseph.

> Then the mother of the sons of Zeb'edee came up to him, with her sons, and kneeling before him she asked him for something. And he said to her, "What do you want?" She said to him, "Command that these two sons of mine may sit, one at your right hand and one at your left, in your kingdom." But Jesus answered, "You do not know what you are asking. Are you able to drink the cup that I am to drink?" They said to him, "We are able." He said to them, "You will drink my cup, but to sit at my right hand and at my left is not mine to grant, but it is for those for whom it has been prepared by my Father" (Mt. 20:20-23).

These places or thrones have been reserved. To sit at Jesus' left or right is a way of signifying those who hold the highest places or thrones in Heaven after Jesus. There can be no question that Our Lady holds the highest place in Heaven after her Son. Thus, it is fitting to place an image of Our Lady beside the Sacred Heart of Jesus after we have enthroned Him. Since Our Lady is the Queen Mother, it is fitting that we think of Mary on a throne beside the King. If we were to take the word "throne" to refer to the most worthy place for Jesus to reside, then we would need to say that the throne is Mary herself. Icons depicting Mary holding the Child Jesus could be said to present Jesus sitting upon His throne.

We don't literally provide a throne in our homes for Jesus and His Mother. Yet we provide a place of honor for the images of Jesus and Mary, which represent their reign of love and mercy over our hearts and over our homes. Again, let us be reminded that the enthronement in the home represents that Jesus is the King of our hearts and that He holds the central place in our hearts. The placement of the image of the Immaculate Heart of Mary in the home represents that Mary is the Queen of our hearts, always leading us to the Heart of Jesus. Of course, each of us must accept the reign of the Hearts of Jesus and Mary over each of our hearts.

28. May the enthronement be accompanied by the placement of an image of St. Joseph in the home?

If we were to place an image of our Blessed Mother and Virgin Queen alongside Jesus our King to His right, could we not place an image of St. Joseph His virgin father to His left? (On the title virgin father, cf. Thomas Aquinas, In Mt. 12:46, In Gal. 1:19). The great dignity of being the virgin father of Jesus has its principle in St. Joseph's marriage to the Blessed Virgin Mary. St. Joseph was able to receive Jesus because he received the Virgin Mary as his wife. Through Our Lady, St. Joseph is more closely united to Jesus than any other human being. After Jesus and Mary, St. Joseph holds the highest place in Heaven. To illustrate this, let us consider two persons from the Old Testament who prefigure St. Joseph, the patriarch Joseph and Mordecai. Let us first look at the patriarch Joseph, a type of St. Joseph. Pope Leo XIII made this comparison in *Quamquam Pluries* (n. 4). We might simply reflect on how a pagan king treated the patriarch Joseph. Then we might reflect on how much more Jesus and Mary would honor Joseph.

The patriarch Joseph prefigures St. Joseph

> So Pharaoh said to Joseph, "Since God has shown you all this, there is none so discreet and wise as you are; you shall be over my house, and all my people shall order themselves as you command; only as regards the throne will I be greater than you." And Pharaoh said to Joseph, "Behold, I have set you over all the land of Egypt." Then Pharaoh took his signet ring from his hand and put it on Joseph's hand, and arrayed him in garments of fine linen, and put a gold chain about his neck; and he made him to ride in his second chariot; and they cried before him, "Bow the knee!" Thus he set him over all the land of Egypt. Moreover Pharaoh said to Joseph, "I am Pharaoh, and without your consent no man shall lift up hand or foot in all the land of Egypt" (Gen. 41:39-44).

Here we see prefigured in the patriarch, the special place of St. Joseph after Jesus and Mary in the Kingdom of God. In addition, scholars suggest that the Gospel of Matthew implies this connection between the two Josephs. Both Josephs have a father named Jacob. Both are guided by multiple dreams. Both are given authority and serve their king. Both care for others and save lives. Yet, the role of St. Joseph surpasses that of anyone after Jesus and Mary. Thus, it is fitting that after the enthronement of the

Section Three

Sacred Heart of Jesus and the placement of the image of the Immaculate Heart of Mary, we place an image of St. Joseph beside Our Lord.

Mordecai prefigures St. Joseph

Yet there is another type or prefigurement of St. Joseph in the Old Testament in the person of Mordecai who interceded with and through Queen Esther, a type of Mary, in order to save the people of Israel. Moreover, we might simply reflect on how a pagan king and a Jewish queen treated Mordecai.

> On that day King Ahasu-e'rus gave to Queen Esther the house of Haman, the enemy of the Jews. And Mor'decai came before the king, for Esther had told what he was to her; and the king took off his signet ring, which he had taken from Haman, and gave it to Mor'decai. And Esther set Mor'decai over the house of Haman....
> Then Mor'decai went out from the presence of the king in royal robes of blue and white, with a great golden crown and a mantle of fine linen and purple, while the city of Susa shouted and rejoiced. The Jews had light and gladness and joy and honor. And in every province and in every city, wherever the king's command and his edict came, there was gladness and joy among the Jews, a feast and a holiday....
> For Mor'decai was great in the king's house, and his fame spread throughout all the provinces; for the man Mor'decai grew more and more powerful....
> For Mor'decai the Jew was next in rank to King Ahasu-e'rus, and he was great among the Jews and popular with the multitude of his brethren, for he sought the welfare of his people and spoke peace to all his people. (Est. Ch. 8, Ch. 10).

If such a worldly king knew how to honor Mordecai, then what are we to say of the King of Kings, Jesus? If Mordecai was able to cooperate in saving his people and earn a place next to the king and Esther, we should not be surprised to see that St. Joseph has done likewise. Fittingly we place his picture in the company of the Hearts of Jesus and Mary.

Fatima and the Book of Esther

It should be noted that Our Lady of Fatima related her appearances to the book of Esther. Our Blessed Mother asked the children to come to the Cova on the 13th of each month for six consecutive months. In the book of Esther, the number 13 appears 6 times. Also, Our Lady appeared each time with a star on her dress. The name Esther means star. Finally, on the 6th month and the 13th of the month, St. Joseph appeared holding the Child Jesus accompanied by the Virgin Mary. Mordecai saved the life of the king and through Esther obtained the salvation of his people. By receiving Mary into his home, Joseph received Jesus. As the guardian of the Redeemer, Joseph saved the life of the little King Jesus. Thus, Jesus lived on in order to redeem us on the Cross. And so, Esther and Mordecai find a higher meaning in the reign of Mary and Joseph, who have brought about and will bring about a great victory for the Lord. Fittingly, then, we place the images of Mary and Joseph in our homes with the enthroned image of the Sacred Heart of Jesus, the Savior of the world. We are again reminded that Jesus told the mother of James and John that to sit at His right or left is not His to give (cf. Mt. 20:23). Who else but Mary and Joseph could sit at the right and at the left of Our Lord in the kingdom of Heaven? It is fitting then to represent this by placing the images of Our Lady and St. Joseph beside the enthroned image of the Sacred Heart of Jesus.

St. Joseph and the thrones of the Apostles

As referred to earlier, Jesus told His disciples, "as my Father appointed a kingdom for me, so do I appoint for you that you may eat and drink at my table in my kingdom, and sit on thrones judging the twelve tribes of Israel" (Lk. 22:29-30). Here we see that the twelve Apostles also sit on thrones. All the more can we speak of both Mary and Joseph being placed beside Jesus on thrones. As mentioned above, Jesus said, "… but to sit at my right hand and at my left is not mine to grant, but it is for those for whom it has been prepared by my Father" (Mt. 20:23). Certainly, it is fitting that St. Joseph receives that second throne beside our Lord as His virgin father and husband of the Queen. Again, keep in mind that the use of the word "thrones" here should not be confused with enthronement which is a term that has been reserved for the Sacred Heart of Jesus.

An approved image

When deciding on an image of St. Joseph to place in the home or other venue, it is important to note that, at this time, we are not aware of any

Section Three

approval by the Church regarding the public use of images bearing the heart of St. Joseph. Thus, we would simply use the images of St. Joseph that are approved at the present time. This does not prevent us from referring to the heart of St. Joseph just as the Sacred Scripture refers to the hearts of all people in general or individually. Also, after Jesus and Mary, the heart of St. Joseph is most chaste and pure. "Blessed are the pure in heart, for they shall see God" (Mt. 5:8). Like Jesus, Joseph's heart is meek and humble. Like Mary, he kept all these things in his heart. We may place Joseph in our hearts as well. As Joseph received Jesus through Mary, so does he lead us to the Heart of Jesus through Mary.

Appendix A

How to Say the Rosary

How to Pray the Rosary

This section called "How to pray the Rosary" is to help those families and individuals unfamiliar with saying the Rosary. One of the elements of the Rosary is the contemplation of the Mysteries "in communion with Mary" (cf. St. Paul VI, Marialis Cultus, n. 49).

The Rosary is ordinarily said in the following manner.

Begin by making the Sign of the Cross.

In the name of the Father, and of the Son, and of the Holy Spirit.

Using Rosary beads, pray the Apostles' Creed holding the Crucifix:

I believe in God, the Father almighty, Creator of heaven and earth, and in Jesus Christ, his only Son, our Lord, who was conceived by the Holy Spirit, born of the Virgin Mary, suffered under Pontius Pilate, was crucified, died and was buried; he descended into hell; on the third day he rose again from the dead; he ascended into heaven, and is seated at the right hand of God the Father almighty; from there he will come to judge the living and the dead.

I believe in the Holy Spirit, the holy catholic Church, the communion of saints, the forgiveness of sins, the resurrection of the body, and life everlasting. Amen.

On the large bead, pray the Our Father (the Lord's Prayer):

Our Father, who art in heaven, hallowed be thy name; thy kingdom come, thy will be done on earth, as it is in heaven. Give us this day, our daily bread, and forgive us our trespasses, as we forgive those who trespass against us; and lead us not into temptation, but deliver us from evil. Amen.

On the next three small beads, pray the Hail Mary:

Hail Mary full of grace, the Lord is with thee; blessed art thou among women, and blessed is the Fruit of thy womb, Jesus. Holy Mary, Mother of God, pray for us sinners now, and at the hour of our death. Amen.

Then pray the Glory Be:

The Pilgrim Virgin Statue Church to Home Visitation

Glory be to the Father, and to the Son, and to the Holy Spirit, as it was in the beginning, is now, and ever shall be, world without end. Amen.

The Mysteries of the Rosary chosen may correspond to the day of the week. Ordinarily, the Mysteries that may be chosen are as follows:

- *The Joyful Mysteries on Mondays and Saturdays.*
- *The Luminous Mysteries on Thursdays.*
- *The Sorrowful Mysteries on Tuesdays and Fridays.*
- *The Glorious Mysteries on Wednesdays and Sundays.*

Announce or call to mind the mystery before each decade. Calling to mind a related Scripture verse or two is recommended by St. John Paul II before each decade (Rosarium Virginis Mariae).

The Joyful Mysteries

The First Joyful Mystery: The Annunciation of the Lord
The Second Joyful Mystery: The Visitation of Mary to Elizabeth
The Third Joyful Mystery: The Birth of Jesus
The Fourth Joyful Mystery: The Presentation of the Child Jesus in the Temple
The Fifth Joyful Mystery: The Finding of the Child Jesus in the Temple

The Luminous Mysteries

The First Luminous Mystery: The Baptism of Our Lord
The Second Luminous Mystery: The Marriage Feast at Cana
The Third Luminous Mystery: The Proclamation of the Gospel
The Fourth Luminous Mystery: The Transfiguration of Jesus Christ
The Fifth Luminous Mystery: The Institution of the Holy Eucharist

The Sorrowful Mysteries

The First Sorrowful Mystery: The Agony of Jesus in the Garden
The Second Sorrowful Mystery: The Scourging of Jesus at the Pillar
The Third Sorrowful Mystery: The Crowning of Jesus with Thorns
The Fourth Sorrowful Mystery: Jesus Carries the Cross

Appendix A

The Fifth Sorrowful Mystery: The Crucifixion and Death of Our Lord

The Glorious Mysteries

The First Glorious Mystery: The Resurrection of Jesus from the Dead

The Second Glorious Mystery: The Ascension of Jesus into Heaven

The Third Glorious Mystery: The Descent of the Holy Spirit upon Mary and the Apostles

The Fourth Glorious Mystery: The Assumption of Mary into Heaven

The Fifth Glorious Mystery: The Crowning of Mary as Queen of Heaven and Earth

On the large bead, pray the Our Father.

On the ten small beads, pray the Hail Mary.

At the end of each decade, pray the Glory Be.

Each decade is followed by the Fatima prayer requested by Our Lady:

O my Jesus, forgive us our sins, save us from the fires of hell; lead all souls to Heaven, especially those in most need of Thy mercy.

Although one is not required to say the above prayer in order to say the Rosary, we recommend the use of this prayer because Our Lady taught the children of Fatima to say this prayer. Our Lady requested that this prayer be said at the end of each decade of the Rosary. Our Lady made this request on July 13, 1917, the same day she spoke of the First Saturdays.

The following is another version of the prayer that might be preferred: "O my Jesus, forgive us, save us from the fire of hell. Lead all souls to Heaven, especially those who are most in need" ("Fatima in Lucia's own words," Dominican Nuns of Perpetual Rosary, p. 179). This is a literal translation from Lucia's own words. Local usage may vary from this translation while sufficiently retaining the original meaning. Thus the popular form may be retained in order to avoid any confusion.

The Pilgrim Virgin Statue Church to Home Visitation

At the end of the five decades, say the Hail Holy Queen.

Hail Holy Queen, Mother of mercy, our life, our sweetness and our hope. To thee do we cry, poor banished children of Eve. To thee do we send up our sighs, mourning and weeping in this vale of tears. Turn then most gracious advocate, thine eyes of mercy towards us, and after this our exile, show unto us the blessed fruit of thy womb, Jesus. O clement, O loving, O sweet Virgin Mary. Pray for us, O holy Mother of God. That we may be made worthy of the promises of Christ.

Let us pray

O God, whose only begotten Son, by His Life, Death, and Resurrection, has purchased for us the rewards of eternal life, grant we beseech thee, that meditating on these Mysteries of the Most Holy Rosary of the Blessed Virgin Mary, we may imitate what they contain, and obtain what they promise, through the same Christ Our Lord. Amen.

Appendix B

Information on the First Saturdays Devotion

Information on the First Saturdays Devotion

1. What did Our Lady of the Rosary at Fatima say God wants?

"You have seen hell where the souls of poor sinners go. In order to save them, God wishes **to establish in the world devotion to my Immaculate Heart**. If you do what I tell you, **many souls will be saved**, there will be **peace**.... I shall come to ask for the consecration of Russia to my Immaculate Heart, and the **Communion of reparation on the first Saturdays**. If my **requests** are fulfilled, Russia will be converted and there will be peace" (July 13, 1917, emphasis ours).

2. What has been done?

The consecration of Russia and the world was fulfilled on March 25, 1984 by St. John Paul II and the bishops of the world.

- This opened the way for the end of the persecution in Russia as Jesus promised Sr. Lucia in 1930, and also for the return of religious freedom in Russia. Many other countries in Eastern Europe have shared in these blessings as well.
- This was the 1st of 2 phases toward Russia's conversion, which is yet to come.

Very few have fulfilled our Lady's second and most important request for the Communion of reparation on the *First Saturdays*.

- The fulfillment of this second and most important request will help bring about the conversion of the world and a period of peace.

3. Pope Benedict XVI's Words at Fatima

"We would be mistaken to think that Fatima's prophetic mission is complete..." (May 13, 2010).

4. What is the Communion of reparation on the First Saturdays? (also known as the First Saturdays or First Saturdays devotion)

On December 10, 1925, Jesus and Mary came to Lucia. Jesus said, "Have compassion on the Heart of your Most Holy Mother covered with the thorns with which ungrateful men pierce it at every moment, and there is no one to remove them with an act of reparation." Mary then said, "My daughter, look at My Heart surrounded with the thorns with which ungrateful men pierce it at every moment by their blasphemies and ingratitude. You at least try to console me, and say that **I promise to assist at the hour of death with all the graces necessary for salvation all those who on the first Saturday of five consecutive months, go to Confession and receive Holy Communion, recite five decades of the Rosary and keep me company for a quarter of an hour while meditating on the mysteries of the Rosary, with the intention of making reparation to me"** (emphasis ours).

5. What are the two promises made by Our Lady in regard to the First Saturdays?

The **1st promise** in regard to the *First Saturdays* was made on July 13, 1917. Our Lady promised the salvation of souls, and a period of peace, together with the conversion of Russia if we fulfill her two special requests. One request remains to be fulfilled, the *First Saturdays*. The first promise requires that we persevere in making the *First Saturdays* and is not limited to making 5 consecutive *First Saturdays*. This first promise also requires that a large number of people fulfill the *First Saturdays*. In this way, we may try to help repair the sins of the world, and in particular, those against the Immaculate Heart of Mary. In this way also, we can remove what prohibits an outpouring of graces through the Immaculate Heart of Mary. Thus, in the ongoing practice of the *First Saturdays*, we can greatly benefit our neighbor as well as ourselves.

On December 10, 1925, Our Lady made a **2nd promise** of salvation for each one who makes the five *First Saturdays* (See the bold print in the previous question.). This 2nd promise presupposes that we are already aware of the 1st promise. In time we should come to realize that the love of the Hearts of Jesus and Mary is our greatest motivation for practicing this devotion.

6. Why are there 5 First Saturdays?

There are 5 *First Saturdays* because, as Jesus told Sr. Lucia, there are 5 kinds of offenses and blasphemies against the Immaculate Heart of Mary:
1. Against the Immaculate Conception of Mary.
2. Against Mary's Virginity.
3. Against Mary's Divine Maternity and her Motherhood of all mankind.
4. Turning children against Mary as their heavenly Mother.

5. Against Mary's Sacred Images.

7. Why is it important to make reparation to the Immaculate Heart of Mary?

Reparation to the Hearts of Jesus and Mary is an act of mercy and an act of justice, which helps repair the harm done by sin. As mentioned above, the Child Jesus said, "Have compassion on the Heart of your Most Holy Mother covered with the thorns with which ungrateful men pierce it at every moment, and there is no one to remove them with an act of reparation." We can try to remove these thorns of sin with acts of reparation to the Immaculate Heart of Mary, not only for our own sins, but also for the sins of others. Also, this reparation can help remove obstacles to the grace and mercy poured out by the Holy Spirit.

Also, because Jesus proclaimed Mary to be our Mother from the Cross when He said, "Behold your Mother!" (Jn. 19:27), we can therefore recognize that she is a Gift to us of His love represented by His Sacred Heart. When Jesus' Gift of Mary is offended, His Heart is offended. Thus, our reparation for the sins against the Immaculate Heart of Mary is essential to a more complete reparation to the Sacred Heart of Jesus. Pope Pius XI wrote of the importance of reparation to the Sacred Heart of Jesus, "And truly the spirit of expiation or reparation has always had the first and foremost place in the worship given to the Most Sacred Heart of Jesus" *(Miserentissimus Redemptor).*

8. What if I start the First Saturdays devotion one month and cannot complete it the next month?

You would need to restart in order to make five consecutive *First Saturdays*. However, even though the one month would not count toward the fulfillment of the five consecutive *First Saturdays*, it can still be of great value, and can benefit one's self and one's neighbor.

9. What if I forget to do one of the practices of the five First Saturdays?

All the practices are necessary to complete each First Saturday. This includes the intention of making reparation to the Immaculate Heart of Mary by each of the four practices. If you forget one practice, you should start again for 5 consecutive *First Saturdays*. Further, hopefully, the faithful will continue to make the *First Saturdays*, beyond five, for peace and the salvation of souls.

10. How do I keep Our Lady company for a quarter of an hour while meditating on the mysteries of the Rosary with the intention of making reparation to her Immaculate Heart?

You can fulfill Our Lady's request for this meditation any time on the *First Saturdays*. If possible, a special time to do this is immediately after Holy Mass in which we can receive Jesus in Holy Communion. One might read and ponder the Scriptures or some other reading about the mysteries of the Rosary while keeping Our Blessed Mother company.

11. Is it all right to meditate on any of the mysteries of the Rosary that one wishes?

There are no requirements as to which mysteries one chooses to meditate on in fulfilling the *First Saturdays*. It would be helpful to plan on covering all of the mysteries over a period of time.

12. What if I cannot go to Confession on the First Saturday?

One can go to Confession anytime as long as there is one Confession for each First Saturday (within about 20 days before or after), and as Jesus said, "as long as they receive Me in the state of grace and have the intention of making reparation to the Immaculate Heart of Mary" (Jesus to Sr. Lucia, 1926).

13. Remember

In order to fulfill the *First Saturdays* devotion, on five consecutive *First Saturdays* and on a continuing basis, the following 4 separate actions must be completed:

1. Go to **Confession** *with the intention of making reparation to the Immaculate Heart of Mary.*
2. Receive **Holy Communion** *with the intention of making reparation to the Immaculate Heart of Mary.*
3. Pray the **Rosary** (5 decades) *with the intention of making reparation to the Immaculate Heart of Mary.*
4. **Keep Our Lady company** for an additional 15 minutes while **meditating** on the mysteries of the Rosary *with the intention of making reparation to the Immaculate Heart of Mary.*

Appendix B

14. Power in Prayer Together

"'Clearly the most efficacious kind of prayer for gaining the divine protection is prayer that is offered publicly by the whole community; for Our Redeemer said: 'Where two or three are gathered...'"(St. John XXIII, *Paenitentiam Agere*, n. 23; cf. also Mt. 18:19-20)

Thus, communal prayer can have a greater power to obtain an answer from God and can have a greater reparatory value. The *Communal First Saturdays* provides these benefits for us.

The *Communal First Saturdays* is a parish or community celebration of the First Saturdays in which all the conditions of the First Saturdays are fulfilled while **joining together** with others in reparation to the Immaculate Heart of Mary.

The *Communal First Saturdays* helps a person fulfill all the conditions of the *First Saturdays* by participating in the parish service on those days. The **Sacrament of Penance** is made available before the service begins. Some helpful prayers related to the Fatima message are said to begin the service followed by the communal recitation of the **Rosary**. The Rosary is prayed before the Holy Mass. The Rosary helps to prepare the faithful for the Holy Mass and the **Communion of reparation**. As St. Paul VI said, the Rosary can be "an excellent preparation" for the Liturgy and "a continuing echo thereof" (*Marialis Cultus*). After the Holy Mass, the faithful keep Our Lord and Our Lady company while making the **15 minute meditation** on Scriptures for two or more mysteries of the Rosary. This is a more special time for the meditation since the faithful would have just received Jesus in Holy Communion.

Also, this meditation is made in a communal form of *lectio divina*. The leader begins the first step of the *lectio divina* by reading a verse or more of Scripture at a time with pauses for reflection by the faithful. The result is that this meditation on the mysteries of the Rosary becomes a "continuing echo" of the Liturgy. It follows that the *Communal First Saturdays* helps us to "Rediscover the Rosary in the light of Scripture, in harmony with the Liturgy, and in the context of [our] daily lives." (St. John Paul II, *Rosarium Virginis Mariae*, n. 43, brackets are ours).

Further, Jesus and Mary made it clear that the First Saturdays can only be fulfilled if each of the above practices is **done with the intention of making reparation to the Immaculate Heart of Mary.**

This communal celebration of the *First Saturdays* offers an **easier way** for people to fulfill the conditions of the *First Saturdays*. Also, the communal celebration offers a service in which a much **larger number of**

people are able to practice the *First Saturdays*, not only for five *First Saturdays*, but on a continual basis. Because of its communal form, the *Communal First Saturdays* gives visible witness that the *First Saturdays* devotion is being practiced. Otherwise, without a communal form, when the time comes, it will be very difficult to connect the *First Saturdays* with the fulfillment of Our Lady's promise of peace. Finally, through the *Communal First Saturdays*, we can make reparation and obtain the graces of conversion for ourselves and others in greater measure, and so can help bring about a period of peace and the salvation of souls.

It is also important to note that the *Communal First Saturdays* is the first canonically approved public *First Saturdays* devotion accompanying the Liturgy in a standardized written form that can be established in any parish. Therefore, we encourage you to use the associated devotional materials available through the Communal First Saturdays Apostolate (contact information included below).

Of special mention, the *Communal First Saturdays Devotional* is a book that makes it easier for the faithful to fulfill each practice of the *First Saturdays* from beginning to end. This book includes preselected Scripture Meditations on the Mysteries of the Rosary for each month of the year to make it easier for the parish and leaders to provide the meditation. Parishes can order enough copies to be passed out every First Saturday for the faithful to use and then be collected.

Please go to our website listed below to order the books and any other materials to help you start or learn more about the *Communal First Saturdays*. For those residing in countries other than the United States, please contact us at info@communalfirstsaturdays.org to order.

"If you do what I tell you, many souls will be saved, there will be peace."
Our Lady of the Rosary at Fatima, July 13, 1917

"Christ will conquer through [Mary], because He wants the Church's victories now and in the future to be linked to her."
St. John Paul II

The above text can be found in the "First Saturdays Devotion" pamphlet, which can be found at www.CommunalFirstSaturdays.org

Appendix C

Hymns

Hymns

These hymns are included here for your convenience. The family or individual is free to choose other appropriate hymns.

Hail, Holy Queen Enthroned Above

Hail, holy Queen enthroned above, O Maria.
Hail, Queen of mercy and of love, O Maria.
Triumph, all ye cherubim, Sing with us, ye seraphim,
Heaven and earth resound the hymn:
Salve, salve, salve Regina!

The cause of joy to men below, O Maria.
The spring through which all graces flow, O Maria.
Angels, all your praises bring, Earth and heaven, with us sing,
All creation echoing:
Salve, salve, salve Regina!

Immaculate Mary

Immaculate Mary, your praises we sing;
You reign now in splendor with Jesus our King.
Ave, ave, ave, Maria! Ave, ave, Maria!

In heaven, the blessed your glory proclaim;
On earth we, your children, invoke your sweet name.
Ave, ave, ave, Maria! Ave, ave, Maria!

We pray for the Church, our true Mother on earth,
And beg you to watch o'er the land of our birth.
Ave, ave, ave, Maria! Ave, ave, Maria!

Contact Information

**For more information or questions, please contact:
Communal First Saturdays Apostolate**
www.CommunalFirstSaturdays.org
Email:
info@communalfirstsaturdays.org

Made in the USA
Middletown, DE
24 July 2022

69751295R00066